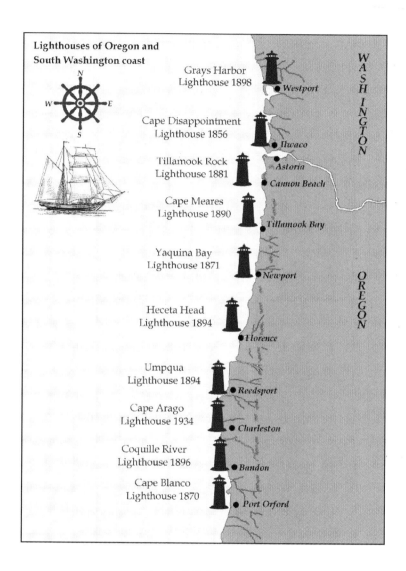

Lighthouses of Oregon and South Washington coast

N
W — E
S

Grays Harbor Lighthouse 1898
● *Westport*

Cape Disappointment Lighthouse 1856
● *Ilwaco*
○ *Astoria*

Tillamook Rock Lighthouse 1881
● *Cannon Beach*

Cape Meares Lighthouse 1890
● *Tillamook Bay*

Yaquina Bay Lighthouse 1871
● *Newport*

Heceta Head Lighthouse 1894
● *Florence*

Umpqua Lighthouse 1894
● *Reedsport*

Cape Arago Lighthouse 1934
● *Charleston*

Coquille River Lighthouse 1896
● *Bandon*

Cape Blanco Lighthouse 1870
● *Port Orford*

W A S H I N G T O N

O R E G O N

Coastal Lighthouses

Lighthouse Keepers Thomas Marshall, James Ducat, Donald McArthur with Lighthouse Board Superintendent Robert Muirhead, about 1890.

Other Duties of Lighthouse Keepers

Tillamook Rock Lighthouse

Brian D. Ratty

Sunset Lake Publishing LLC
89637 Lakeside Ct.
Warrenton, OR 97146
503.717.1125
Brian@Sunsetlakepublishing.com

First Edition published March 2018 – Second Edition June 2018
ISBN-13: 978-0692054819 (Sunset Lake Publishing LLC)
ISBN-10: 0692054812
Create Space Title ID: 7978556
Printed in the USA

This book is dedicated to James A. Gibbs, (January 17, 1922 – April 30, 2010), who as a young Coast Guardsman in 1945 spent tours of duty as a lighthouse Keeper at the Tillamook Rock Lighthouse. In 1948 Mr. Gibbs helped found the Puget Sound Maritime Historical Society and was one of the editors of 'Marine Digest' magazine. In 1979 he published: 'Tillamook Light', his first book about the 77 year history of the Tillamook Rock Lighthouse, also called Terrible Tilly. Over his long career, James also studied, wrote and published many other excellent books about the maritime history of the Pacific Northwest.

The author also dedicates this book to all the 'Keepers of the Light', who helped build, maintain and manned their stations. These were a special breed of men, who lived in danger to prevent others from falling prey to the perils of the sea or shore.

TILLAMOOK ROCK LIGHT

January 1881 – September 1957

Author's Note

I am not an expert on lighthouses. My fascination with Tilly is rooted in my personal experiences and my family's connection to the Rock.

The Tillamook Rock Lighthouse has been called many names by many people. Some called it a 'hoodoo light.' Others called it 'Tilly' or just 'TR', while still others said it was another Government boondoggle. But all agreed it was the loneliest station on earth. Whatever the name, I first recall hearing the hollow howl of its foghorn when I was just a toddler living in Seaside, Oregon during World War II. It frightened me. I ran to my father and asked him what was that growl? He smiled and told me not to worry; it was just Terrible Tilly clearing her throat.

At the time, I had no idea what a Terrible Tilly was, nor did I know that a few years before, my grandfather had almost been killed on Tillamook Rock. (His story is included within this volume.) Now, many years later, with great appreciation, I am honored to be writing the history and tales of Terrible Tilly.

Those of us who lived here in Seaside at the time remember the light well. Its bright beacon and foghorn were as normal to us as the sea and the waves. Little did I realize the importance of this isolated sentinel. Tilly was perched on her rock, a mile out to sea, helping to keep the sea lanes open and our seafarers safe from the many rocks and shoals of the North Oregon Coast.

Tillamook Rock Lighthouse was classed as one of the three most isolated stations of the Lighthouse Service. The other west coast light so classified was St. George Reef Lighthouse, six miles northwest of Crescent City, California. That tall, gray, castle-like structure, 146 feet tall, cannot usually be seen from the mainland. Activated on December, 1891, it cost $721,000 to build, which was about seven times the cost of the Tillamook Light.

St. George Reef Lighthouse

The third light was Minot's Ledge Lighthouse, one mile offshore of Massachusetts. The first lighthouse was built between 1847 and 1850, and was lit in January 1850. One night in April 1851, the new lighthouse was struck by a major storm which caused almost total destruction to the structure and took the lives of two of its Keepers. The replacement tower that was built came back online in November, 1860, at a cost of $330,000. Factoring in the cost of the first light, Minot's Ledge also cost seven times as much to build as the Tillamook light.

Minot's Ledge Lighthouse

Today, the crumbling, nostalgic Tillamook Rock Lighthouse is viewed by tens of thousands of visitors from Seaside, Cannon Beach and Ecola State Park, many of whom wonder why this lone sentinel is standing guard over their vacations. Most don't realize that Tilly is a symbol of man's relentless fight against the cruelties of the sea. This is her true story, filled with challenges and triumphs, courage and hope.

Coast Guard buoy tender with abandoned
lighthouse in the background

Since 1792, almost two thousand large ships have sunk,
in and around the mouth of the Columbia River

CONTENTS

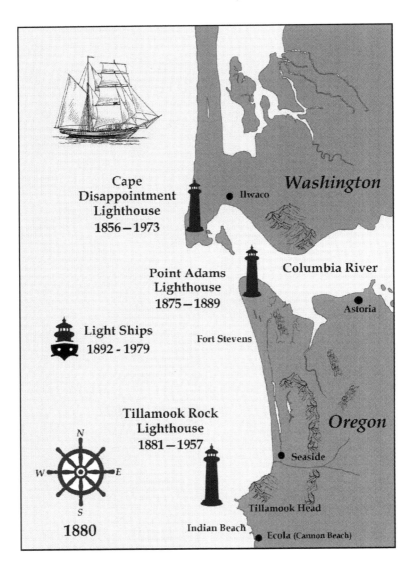

Cape
Disappointment
Lighthouse
1856 – 1973

Ilwaco

Washington

Point Adams
Lighthouse
1875 – 1889

Columbia River

Astoria

Light Ships
1892 - 1979

Fort Stevens

Tillamook Rock
Lighthouse
1881 – 1957

Oregon

N
W — E
S

Seaside

Tillamook Head

1880

Indian Beach

Ecola (Cannon Beach)

Columbia River Bar

Tillamook Rock Lighthouse
History and Tales of Terrible Tilly
Chapter One

Why Tilly?

The Columbia River Bar, where the brackish waters of the river meet the salt waters of the Pacific Ocean, is only three miles wide and six miles long. This stretch of unabated fury, with tall, curling waves and ever-changing rip tides, is considered the second-most-dangerous Bar crossing in the world. Only the entrance to the Amazon River is said to be more treacherous. Since 1792, almost 2000 large ships have sunk, in and around the mouth of the river. Because of these extreme tides, howling winds, and pea-soup fogs, the Columbia Bar has acquired its rightful reputation as the Graveyard of the Pacific.

Back in the days of sailing, it was not uncommon for seafarers to approach the entrance to the river and then lay-off their ships until the weather, winds, and tides were right. At times, crews waited for days or even weeks before crossing the Bar. Long before any navigational aids, Chinook and Clatsop Indians would row their sea canoes out to those ships, offering their services to guide the seafarers safely across the entrance, missing the many rocks, sandbars, and shoals. These Native Mariners were common on the Columbia River, and were the harbingers of the Columbia River Bar Pilots that still thrive today.

From miles out at sea, the entrance to the river is well disguised and hard to find. For many decades, European

Mariners sailed up and down the coast, looking for a mighty river to the east. But they never found it. The river was finally discovered by Yankee sea Captain Robert Gray on his second voyage to the northwest, in 1792. Long before Lewis and Clark, Captain Gray and his crew charted the lower reaches of the river and named it after his ship, *Columbia*.

In the early days of Fort Astoria, men would paddle across the river and set up observation points on the tall mountain on the north side of the entrance. When they saw a ship approaching, they would light large bonfires to signal the ship to the mouth of the river. The smoke and glow from those flames were the first beacons used to guide seafarers safely to land.

Cape Disappointment Lighthouse

In 1856, the first real lighthouse was built on that same mountain top, known today as Cape Disappointment. At the time of its construction, Oregon was still only a Territory, and the U.S. Congress made appropriations of $53,000 to build this first light in the Pacific Northwest.

Point Adams Lighthouse

The second lighthouse, Point Adams, was built across the river from Cape Disappointment, on the southern shore of the Columbia River Bar, in 1875. The Keeper's quarters and light were combined into the wooden structure of the tower.

With the combination of Point Adams and Cape Disappointment, the river entrance was effectively framed with two different warning lights and two different sounding fog horns.

But these improvements weren't enough. Ships still missed the entrance and ran aground. A third light was needed so that the approaching vessels could take navigational bearings to pin-point the mouth of the Columbia River. Rumors about a third light and its location circulated on the thriving Astoria waterfront. Many speculated that the new beacon would be positioned close to the mouth of the river, while others looked to the hills and mountains to the north and south.

The first Colonial American aid to navigation was a light erected in Massachusetts in 1673. That first beacon was erected using rubble stone on Little Brewster Island in Boston Harbor. The light's first Keeper was George Worthylake, he was paid the princely sum of fifty pounds a year. Other Colonies also constructed lighthouses using rubble stone towers, prior to the Revolution. The Customs Collectors of the ports near the light-houses collected "light dues" based on the tonnage of vessels using the ports.

Following independence, the Ninth Act of the first Congress, on August 7, 1789, provided for the transfer of the 12 existing lighthouses from the individual states to the Federal Government, and established a Lighthouse Board as an agency of the Department of the Treasury. This Board became the Lighthouse Service, which was responsible for the construction and maintenance of all lighthouses and navigational aids in the United States. In 1939, the Lighthouse Service was dissolved, and all of its duties were taken over by the Coast Guard.

Prior to the construction of a third lighthouse for the Columbia River, the Lighthouse Service sent out representatives in 1877 to determine the light's location. Their mission was to survey the area, and to talk with mariners about the correct positioning of the lighthouse.

Graphics: Brian D. Ratty
Tillamook Head 1877 Looking ENE

It was soon decided that a large, forested promontory, some 20 miles south of the river, would make the best location. This headland of steep, rocky bluffs rises up over 1200 hundred feet at its peak, with an unobstructed view of the Pacific Ocean. The foreland is a natural travel barrier; years before, it had been the unofficial border between two rival Indian tribes, the Clatsops to the north and the Tillamooks to the south. (Captain Robert Gray discovered the Tillamook Indians on his first voyage to the northwest in 1788.)

The locals called this remote and inaccessible land Tillamook Head. The Lewis and Clark Expedition crossed the formidable headland in 1806 to buy the blubber of a stranded whale from the Indians. They were the first white men to traverse this spectacular and primitive rainforest.

Fortunately for the Lighthouse Representatives, the fore-land was close to the small town of Seaside, Oregon, which offered them some comfort and lodging.

As these hardy surveyors packed in their instruments and supplies, and trudged through the tall, dark Sitka Spruce and Alders of the promontory, they begin to notice what the locals had warned them about. The very top of the Tillamook Head, where they hoped to build the lighthouse, was almost always shrouded in fog or clouds.

They soon abandoned this first position and moved farther south. When they arrived at the other side of headland, they found another possible location, not as high up on the Head, but with a clear view to the ocean. Upon further investigation, however, they determined that the site was unusable because of the high cost of building and maintaining a twenty-mile wagon road over the mountainous terrain for transportation of the construction materials and supplies. Additionally, they questioned the stability of the rock formations at the second site. During their rainy stay on the headlands, they had seen a third option: a large, high rock a mile offshore from the Head. This location looked promising, and would have to be explored by sea.

Ecola State Park and Indian Beach
are the closest landfall to the Rock

Chapter Two

The Rock

Upon reading the reports of the survey done on Till-amook Head, the Lighthouse Board came to the conclusion that the large Rock, one mile off shore of the Head, was the only promising location for the light. They made this decision even though the Rock would have no nearby mainland access and had not yet been properly surveyed. The Board ordered the local District Inspector to perform such a preliminary survey when weather conditions allowed.

The winter of 1878-1879 was especially stormy, and the District Inspector could not find a vessel willing to brave the Bar conditions to begin his survey. It wasn't until early June that he secured a lighthouse tender and crossed the Bar with a crew that knew the area he wished to inspect. But sea conditions were still dicey. The Inspector stood on the deck of the tender, as the boat approached the Rock with great caution. The ship would only go as close as the Captain would allow. The Inspector's official report included this statement:

The ocean swells were so great as to forbid my landing. I was enabled to approach sufficiently near to become convinced that the rock is large enough, and the only suitable place for the light. To be efficient, the light should be exhibited as low as it is safe to have it; the headland is entirely too high on the lowest bench... Though I could not make a landing at the time of my examination, I am of the opinion that it is practicable to use the rock for a light station, and I am desirous of being allowed to make the attempt.

Back in Washington, the Lighthouse Board appointed Mr. H.S. Wheeler as Superintendent of Construction for the new light. He was ordered to Astoria with the understanding that he would not return to headquarters until he was able to actually land on the rock and make the required measurements. But on his arrival to Astoria he found that the lighthouse tender was out to sea and unavailable. The local Collector of Customs, who knew of the proposed light, heard about his predicament and lent him the use of the 140-foot, 227-ton, steam and sail Revenue Cutter *Thomas Corwin,* with Lt. Brann commanding.

The Revenue Cutter Thomas Corwin was a famous ship plying the waters of Alaska for many years

Revenue Cutters were armed Customs enforcement vessels that interdicted illegal whiskey trafficking, game poachers and smugglers. They were part of the Treasury Department, with the mission of collecting taxes from illicit activities. The *Corwin* spent most of her 23-year federal career sailing the Pacific Northwest and Alaskan waters.

With rolling white caps and a howling wind, the *Corwin* crossed the Columbia River Bar on June 22, 1879, and set course for Tillamook Rock.

When the ship arrived at the Rock, they found a moderate sea running on an incoming tide, with waves braking around the base of the monolith. Conditions looked promising, and preparations were made for landing.

The surf boat was lowered and manned by a husky rowing crew, as well as Mr. Wheeler. The men rowed the boat close to shore on the east side and were able to land two men. The weather changed abruptly, and the first two men on shore were unable to do any measurements because the sea started to rise with the coming of a storm. The surf boat approached many times, but could not pick up the stranded sailors. All the shore party could do was jump into the freezing ocean, to be pulled back into the surf boat by their shipmates. Luckily, no lives were lost, although this first experience of landing on the rock would start its infamous reputation as 'Terrible Tilly'.

On June 26th, Wheeler set out again with the *Corwin* to attempt another landing. This time, the sea was too rough to land his surveying instruments, but the Superintendent was successful in gaining a foothold on the Rock, where he made basic measurements of the monolith using a pocket tape. He included this information in his official report dated June 30, 1879:

This is an isolated basaltic rock divided above low-water level into two very unequal parts by a wide fissure with vertical sides running east and west, stands 100 feet approx. above the sea and has a crest [top] which is capable of being reduced so as to accommodate a structure not greater than fifty feet square.... Though the execution of the work will be a task of labor and difficulty, accompanied with great expense, yet the benefits to the commerce seeking the mouth of the Columbia River will derive from a light and fog signal located there will warrant all the labor and expense involved.

The water on the west, north and east sides of the rock is from 25 to 40 fathoms deep but shoals to 16 or 18 fathoms on the south over a limited area. Midway between this rock and the Head is a small rock awash at low tide over which the sea breaks heavily during storms. Tillamook Rock raises from the sea on the west in a precipitous manner for about 15 feet then breaks under a gentle, irregular slope for a short distance forming a narrow bench that embraces part of the south face and all of the west and north faces.

On the west side, arising from this bench with a marked inclination seaward, the rock rises to 80 feet and is terminated at its crest by a large rounded knob (head) resembling the burl of a tree. This overhang is about 25 feet long on a west to east position. On the north is a vertical wall above the bench near the water's edge. The east side is very steep and irregular from the top to a level of 30 feet below then it slopes to the sea at about 20 percent angle. There is a deep fissure (crack) about 25 feet wide on the south side that divides the rock into two unequal parts. From the surface of the sea, the rock here rises gradually to about 30 feet above the sea where it is abruptly closed by a wall of rock which forms part of the east slope of the main rock. During storms, waves break with great violence into this fissure throwing spray all the way to the top of the rock and down the other side.

Fissure

Photo: Brian D. Ratty

This separate rock or fissure, isolated from the main rock, formed a tall, narrow spine with sharp, pointed crags about 50 feet high. In many ways, Tillamook Rock looked like the hump of a camel's back. There was not a single blade of grass growing on the island and the drawing of the

Rock which Mr. Wheeler included with his report is the only illustration of what it looked like before the coming of the lighthouse. Folklore stories of long ago told about both the Clatsop and Tillamook Indians visiting the Rock in their sea canoes to gather bird eggs and kill sea lions for their hides. At the time when Mr. Wheeler made his survey, he noted that it was crawling with sea lions that quickly went back into the ocean upon his approach. The locals also said the waters around the bastion were rich with bottom fish and crabs. One can only imagine how many Keepers enjoyed meals of fresh fish stew caught right off their Rock.

Tillamook Rock drawing included with official government report

Before and After Decapitation

His detailed report also clearly established that there was no suitable portage on the Rock due to ever-changing sea conditions and many hidden underwater rocky ledges. Mr. Wheeler looked for a suitable moorage on the mainland, east of the Rock. He found none. The closest place where a small boat might land was in a small, sandy cove northeast of the island. Therefore, all supplies and construction materials would have to be shipped in from Astoria. Somehow, they would have to devise a way to unload supplies and men from the ships to the Rock.

Back in Washington, Congress started the process of funding the new lighthouse. On June 20, 1878, the sum of 50 thousand dollars was appropriated out of any monies in the Treasury not otherwise appropriated, for the purpose of constructing a *first-class* lighthouse on Tillamook Head, Oregon.

The Lighthouse Board made two additional requests for funding: on June 16, 1880, for 25 thousand dollars for the continuing erection of a *first-class* lighthouse and fog signal on Tillamook Head, Oregon, and on March 3, 1881, for 25 thousand dollars for completing the erection of a *first-class* lighthouse and *steam fog signal* on the Rock off Tillamook Head, Oregon.

Note: the term *first-class*, which denotes that the light used for the beacon will only be of the finest quality of optics and mirrors. (Also note that only the last appropriations had the correct location of the lighthouse.) The total cost to the Government to build Tillamook Rock Lighthouse was estimated at $100,000, a handsome sum for the day.

Shipwrecks

Chapter Three

Decapitation

On July 11, 1879, the Lighthouse Board received a report with preliminary plans and estimates for building the necessary structures for a light station on the Rock.

The plan called for a small crew of workers, eight to ten men, to be housed on the monolith with provisions, tools, and canvas tents for four to five months, with the purpose of decapitating the top of the Rock. Their mission was to blast away the rock, using black powder, until a level platform could be realized on which structures could be built. The powder monkeys were instructed to take great care to keep the level area as large and as high above the boiling sea as possible. The imperfect measurements taken by Mr. Wheeler indicated that the main building should be at least 88 feet above mean low tide.

Other plans were put in motion to have all building materials, heavy machinery, derricks, and miscellaneous supplies marshaled to Astoria for transfer to the Rock when the site was ready. Nearly all of the materials used in the construction of the lighthouse came from Oregon sources.

Two years before, in August of 1877, the Secretary of State for Oregon transferred the title of the Tillamook Rock to the United States Government with this property description: ...an isolated basaltic rock, known as Tillamook Rock, standing in the Pacific Ocean one mile seaward of the most westerly point of Tillamook Head, Clatsop County, Oregon and 20 miles, approx.. south of the

Columbia River Bar in NW quarter Sec 11 Twnsp 5N., R 11
W. Willamette Meridian...&tc.

With the single stroke of a pen, Tillamook Rock went
from the hands of Mother Nature into the grasp of the
Lighthouse Board. It would never be the same again.

With schedules underway and materials being pro-
cured, the Lighthouse Board realized that the original
measurements had been done in haste and only made with a
hand line. They knew it was necessary to have an official
survey done before construction started. With this in mind,
a Master Mason, Mr. John R. Trewavas of Portland, was
hired. He came highly qualified and had earlier worked
building lighthouses in England.

The Revenue Cutter was again commandeered, with
the intentions of landing the master mason and his assistant
on the Rock. When the ship arrived at the site, and the surf
boat approached the monolith in long, rolling swells,
disaster struck. Mr. Trewavas slipped on the wet, slimy
rock and was instantly swept into churning waters. His
assistant jumped into the frigid ocean in a rescue attempt as
the crew of the surf boat threw hand lines out for both men.
The assistant was soon hauled from the waters, but the
mason was pulled down by the undertow and his body
never recovered. Mr. Trewavas was just 38 years old at the
time of the accident. This first death on the Rock was a
chilling reminder of how unforgiving the sea could be.

The news of the mason's death circulated on Astoria's
waterfront, and made many leery of the Tillamook light
project. Superintendent Wheeler wrote of the incident:

This most unfortunate disaster prejudiced the public
against the project of even attempting to land upon this
sea-swept rock, not to speak of building a light-house

there. It became necessary, after the death of [Mr. Trewavas] to act vigorously before the public mind became so diseased by frequent discussions of the dangers of the place as to render abortive the employment of laborers for the undertaking.

The local Astoria newspaper reported on the accident and continued to raise questions about the safety of the project. To placate these concerns, the Lighthouse Board hired Mr. Charles A. Ballantyne, retaining him as a new Construction Superintendent. He was ordered to hire eight or ten skilled quarrymen and blacksmiths in Portland who would report to Astoria, where transportation would take them out to the rock. Once they had landed on the job site, quarters were to be arranged for the men, who were to start the work immediately.

But this order required the use of a steam ship, which would be needed for months to complete the construction of the lighthouse. So the Lighthouse Board back, in Washington, sent a personal representative to see the Secretary of the Treasury and pleaded with him for the steamship *Corwin* to be temporarily assigned to that duty. This was accomplished in September of 1879.

That autumn found constant strong southwesterly winds blowing across the Columbia River Bar. The waters were so rough that no ship could make the passage out to sea. This delay worried the new Superintendent, for he could not risk having his newly hired men come into contact with the malicious gossip in Astoria about the safety of the project. Therefore, in a desperate move, Ballantyne shipped his entire crew across the river, where they occupied the old Light Keeper's quarters at Fort Canby, near Cape Disappointment.

On October 12, the *Corwin* cleared the Bar in rolling seas and set course for the Rock. When the ship arrived at the isolated monolith, they put down mooring buoys on the north and east sides of the site in 25 fathoms of water. Here they waited out a storm and made plans for how the work would proceed. A few days later, four quarrymen were successfully landed from the bow of the surf boat, with hammers, drills, and iron ring-bolts to establish safety lines. They also took a large supply of canvas to construct a tent to shelter themselves and to protect their supplies. Other items taken ashore from the surf boat included a stove, food, and protective clothing. The weather was monstrous, with an almost constant blow in driving rain squalls. Five days later, additional workers were landed with more supplies and a small derrick. The official date of commencing work was October 26, 1879. One of the first improvements these crews made was the construction of a privy that clung on the precipice of the rock like a conical shell, 80 feet directly over the ocean.

After this initial experience of landing workers and supplies, the Superintendent realized that a more efficient way of transferring men and materials from the ship to the shore had to be found.

On the journey back to Astoria, Ballantyne and Lt. Brann consulted on safer ways of unloading cargo onto the job site. When the *Corwin* returned, a few days later, they put their new plan into action. The ship moored at one of the spar buoys, about 300 feet offshore from the Rock.

The surf boat was launched, manned by muscular sailors and two blacksmiths. Both men gained a foothold on the Rock and scrambled up the slippery surface to a safe place. The boat returned to the cutter and took the end of a small line, attached to a bigger rope that had its end tied high to the mast of the vessel. The end of the small line was run out with the surf boat to the Rock, where the blacksmiths pulled it across the water, dragging the larger rope with it. The men fastened the larger rope into the basaltic rock, using large ring-bolts with iron anchors hammered into the stone. This rigged cable from ship to shore was 85 feet above the water, and it became the supply line for men and materials. A large wooden bin or "traveler" was attached to the cable, using a system of pulleys which could be loaded and pulled over to the monolith and then pulled back to the ship for more cargo.

This method of using a rope gondola was much more efficient and far safer for moving men and supplies between the ship and the Rock. There was a risk that some of the loaded goods, as well as some of the men being carried on the line, would get a dragging through the water, because the ship to which one end of the cable was attached rose and fell with the swells of the sea. While most supplies were merely lashed into the box and exposed to the weather, articles that could be damaged by water were placed in sealed casks and hauled over this aerial tram with relative safety. When it came to the transport of workers, each man was placed in a "breeches buoy" and hauled by a system of pulleys between the craft and the Rock. Often, these men got a dunking into the cold sea when traveling across the cable.

This system of moving workers was not the best, but there seemed to be no other way that afforded such a high degree of safety, compared with the attempts to land men by using the surf boat. As soon as this jury-rigged transport system was installed, three more men were sent to the Rock, as well as loads of supplies including enough fresh water to last one month. By nightfall, the seas started boiling, so the ship returned to Astoria.

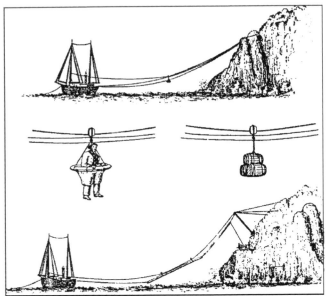

Government sketches: (top) The Corwin anchored to a spar-buoy
about 300 feet from the rock. After careful and dangerous work. Lines
were run between the ship and shore. (middle left) A "traveler" was
rigger on which men, in breeches buoy were moved to and from the
rock. (middle right) Supplies, especially barrels of drinking water,
were hauled on the "traveler" to the monolith. (bottom) The ship,
anchored at the buoy, is landing the log boom for the first derrick.
Some of which has already been completed.

With winter fast approaching, and men and materials
safely on the Rock, all seemed ready for a productive time
on the job site. But progress would depend wholly on the
weather. Before any work could be attempted, it was
necessary for the landed party to construct living quarters.
There were no outcroppings or deep recesses where a
shelter could be built. And it rained. And the wind blew.
And the sea kicked up salty spray that seemed to penetrate
everything and everyone. In the wet, it was impossible to
get a fire going in the coal stove, so food was cold, and the
men had no heat. Working conditions were dismal, and the

workers were virtually marooned on this wet, cold, miserable monolith.

The men cut up some of the canvas for a shelter and set up a few make-shift A-frame tents. These were lashed to the ring bolts that had been set into the rock. Under these horrible weather conditions, and with great effort, they managed to clear and level an area about 90 feet above the sea, on the south side. Here they hoped to build a small framed house for living quarters, but a raging sea sprayed the area through the fissure, quickly indicating that the site was unusable. They soon abandoned the area in favor of another spot on the north side.

When this new site was leveled, and the crew was relatively safely quartered, work commenced at the 30 foot elevation for a derrick. Soon, a crude path was chiseled out of the rock, connecting the derrick and the quarters. All of this took time, in the face of discouraging weather. The official report provides the following insights as to how the work got underway:

The manner of working, at first, was to suspend a boatswain's chair from a ring bolt at the summit, along the steep side down to the grade level. The boatswain's chair was formed of a short board secured with ropes on each end. A quarryman, sitting in this chair, would both strike and turn a short drill. And a man would be similarly suspended, without a chair but with a safety rope tied to him so that, if his foot slipped, he would be prevented from falling into the sea. By either method, a man would drill shallow "breast holes," from 12 to 18 inches deep and 4 inches diameter, running directly into the face of the rock. Small blasting cartridges of not over one pound of black powder were then inserted into these holes.

Small ledges were also blasted in the face of the rock so that men could stand on them to pursue their work. Soon, at the 90 foot elevation, the masons cut and blasted out a narrow path around the top of the rock. Winds from storm driven gales, even on the lee side of the rock, forced the men to position themselves safely against the wind before they could make any progress. The plan had been to work at the 90 foot level but, because of the weather conditions, an alternate plan was put forward: they would work on the lower level, chipping away until the top was finally reached. The official report relates the story:

The work was enabled to progress by supporting the parties on the levels to be reached upon staging, suspended from bolt attachments set into the crest of the rock. As soon as a bench was made of a sufficient width [on which the men could stand], the parties were concentrated on the leeward side and the reduction was pushed towards the center, gaining at each step in advance a better working place. The outer surface of the rock was covered with thin scales and chipped off rather easily with moderate charges of blasting powder. The nucleus [of the rock] was very firm and tough and the black powder could make but little impression upon it but by opening the mass with giant cartridges and then using large charges of black powder, the rock was blasted.

All through this work, the men were constantly harassed by the weather and their minimally acceptable living conditions. But these were a special breed of men with that can-do attitude of the day. They did their jobs with courage and dedication, and with little or no grumbling.

A major storm visited the coast, early that winter, causing huge green sea waves to crash upon the Rock. The chasm on the south side filled with a boiling sea, and the winds blew the water entirely over the Rock many times. This descent of green sea rushed down the opposite slope and carried away the supply house and all that was in it at the 30-foot level. It also endangered the quarters of the men. The storm reached its maximum strength during the night of the 9th of January, when the men were all in their bunks. One of the men trapped on this pyramid of basalt later wrote of the heroic conduct of Mr. Ballantyne during the storm:

By his determined action he arrested a panic which had seized upon the men and prevented them from deserting their little house for an apparently securer refuge on a higher level in an attempt which would inevitably have led to their destruction as the darkness was intense and the wind most violent. The superintendent had been instructed not to keep many supplies in the supply house on the lower landing but had not yet been able to secure a better place nevertheless, he had stored, in quarters, plenty of hard bread, coffee and bacon to last the company, with some economy in usage, for several weeks.

The storm was felt all along Oregon's northwest coast. Even after the storm subsided, the Bar at the Columbia River was too rough for the ship to cross to bring any relief to the men on their rocky prison. Finally, on January 25, after 16 days of delay and suspense as to the fate of those at Tillamook Rock, the ship steamed to the monolith and found every person safe, though in want of fresh provisions.

With the improving weather after the storm, the work was pushed forward with great vigor. The work force of 10 men was divided for specific duties. A blacksmith spent full time keeping bits sharpened. These bits were of the finest English steel and required re-sharpening after every 2 inches of penetration into the rock. It took two assistants for each man doing the drilling, while the rest of the force was fully occupied pushing the blasted rubble off the perch and into the sea. (The disposal of this rubble would prove to be a great mistake that would cause difficulties for many years to come.)

As the masons were able to work their way to the top of the Rock, they drilled deeper breast holes, 3 inches in diameter. Into these holes were placed 12 to 15 pounds of black powder. The holes were filled and tamped firmly with sand. A fuse and blasting cap of fulminate of mercury was used to ignite the powder. The effects of the explosions opened large fractures in the stone, where more black powder was then placed. These explosions, one by one, brought down over 200 cubic yards of splintered rock, some of it falling into the sea, other rock clogging the benches.

By the end of May, 1880, the decapitation was done and the site was ready for the construction of the light-house. To this point, the work had taken 224 days, during which time 4,630 cubic yards of solid basalt rock had been blasted and chipped away. The level surface was 29.6 feet below the highest point of the original summit. The blasting consumed over 1500 pounds of black powder. The cost for labor and materials, including the chartered ship, was $13, 537.15 or $2.86 for each cubic yard of rock removed.

But, more importantly, there were no reports of any casualties or major injuries during this phase of construction. One can only imagine how absolutely delighted the masons and blacksmiths were to get off that miserable monolith, after over seven months in hell!

Graphic: Brian D. Ratty

Over 1500 pounds of black powder
was used to decapitate the Rock

The Abandoned Station Today

Shipwrecks

Chapter Four

Building the Station

The first order of business, before construction could begin, was to prepare the site to receive massive amounts of building materials and supplies. To accomplish this, a much larger derrick was positioned at the 90 foot level, near the outer face of the Rock. This apparatus was fixed deep into the crag with cement pilings, and functioned as a second derrick. It was rigged with large blocks and tackles, assisted by the traveler and cables. This was the means by which the heavy mast and boom of the lower principal derrick were hoisted into position.

Next to the chiseled out rock steps on the lower level, and leading up to the building site, a tramway was built. Iron tracks were bolted into the rock with a track gauge of 36 inches. These tracks extended from the lower cargo landing area to the north side of the fog-signal room, next to the coal storage bin. Attached to these tracks was a wood and steel gondola 84 inches long and 36 inches wide. This car could be pulled up the tramway by steel cables that were hand cranked from the 90 foot level. Between the two derricks and this new tram, all the construction materials could be hoisted into position.

When the new steam donkey engine arrived, it provided the power to lift men and heavy materials off the decks of the supply ships with ease. This engine was positioned on the 44 foot level between the two derricks, and worked both apparatuses without difficulty and without accident for the entire construction period.

All these activities for heavy lifting were in preparation for the delivery of materials and personnel to build the station. On the docks of Astoria, barges and ships were arriving with tons of ashlar stone, thousands of burnt bricks, bags of mortar and cement, yards of clean pit sand and hundreds of cubic feet of rubble stone. Along with the delivery of these shipments, George Lewis Gillespie, Jr., Head Lighthouse Engineer, arrived from the District Lighthouse Board in San Francisco. He immediately started a careful inspection of all the building materials for quality and quantity, as per Government specifications. Selected stones and bricks were measured and tested for strength. The pit sand was especially scrutinized, to be certain it was free of any dirt. Clean sand was essential in the mortar mix to make the joints strong and weather-tight. All of the Inspectors had been furnished with detailed drawings of each course of the masonry, with dimensions carefully calculated. They marked each stone with numbers and detailed instructions of where the stone should be placed.

At the end of all the inspections, Superintendent Wheeler noted the fine workmanship and timing of all the materials delivered. Almost none had to be rejected before being transported to the Rock.

While these inspections were being made, other representatives from the Lighthouse Board were recruiting more stone masons, blacksmiths, carpenters, and laborers to build the station during the summer months. There are no records to show that any of the original masons or blacksmiths signed up for the construction phase. They must have been done with the Rock!

With the coming of spring, the weather conditions rapidly improved, and the Revenue Cutter *Corwin* was called back to her normal duties as a floating tax collector. With her departure, new supply ships would have to be chartered.

Superintendent Ballantyne determined that small vessels served the purpose of supplying Tillamook Rock better than larger ships, due to the inshore currents around the monolith. These currents separated on reaching the Rock and swept around it on both sides, with such velocities that only small vessels could lie in close enough to the shore for unloading materials. Studies also found that steamers were preferable to sailing ships. This had to do with the distance between the site and Astoria, and particularly from the Columbia River Bar. Many people associated Astoria with the mouth of the Columbia River, but the city is 12 miles upriver from the Bar. The Superintendent's official report discussed the Bar in this manner:

The Columbia River Bar is never very quiet and often breaks so heavily that it cannot be crossed for days when a heavy fog exists either by steamers or sail, and it is a rare occurrence that any sailing vessel is able to cross either way without the assistance of a tug. A sailing vessel as a means of transportation would therefore have been not very expensive but very irregular and uncertain. The peculiar location of Astoria, and its distance from the Bar, prevents a vessel in port from determining the character of the Bar or the sea outside, and often times steamers before going out seek an anchorage in Baker's Bay and there await a favorable crossing. These conditions made the transportation of materials a particularly embarrassing and perplexing one. When the weather was fair, four or five trips were made in a month but often the number was reduced to only one per month. When caught outside [the Bar] and prevented from coming in on account of roughness of the Bar, the vessel was compelled to weather the storm until a favorable opportunity presented for crossing in. To overcome these complexities, the *Mary Taylor* was chartered.

The steam schooner *Mary Taylor* was chartered for general transport between Astoria and Tillamook Rock. The ship was actually a 'sloop-rigged steam tug boat only 67 feet long, 18 feet of beam, with a shallow draft. The *Mary Taylor* could hold six knots in quiet water. Her deck capacity was very limited, and she was not rigged for carrying or hoisting heavy freight. The ship was leased for $1,200 each month. The term of the charter ran until May 20, 1880, when she was replaced with the steam vessel *George Harley*, under the command of Captain J. W. Dodge. This ship was equipped with a large derrick; therefore it was no task to hoist the quarry blocks and heavy sacks of rubble stone and sand from the dock to the ship. At the site, the new large derrick lifted this freight from the ship to the site.

Tillamook Station Under Construction

The steam ship *Shubrick* was the official lighthouse tender for the west coast. She had been built at the Philadelphia Navy Yard with the left-over materials from the construction of the warship *USS Wabash*: a steam screw frigate of the United States Navy that served during the Civil War. The *Shubrick* was topped off with a flush deck, fore and aft, and her hull was painted black, with red paddle wheels, white paddle boxes, and a black bowsprit. But she was unavailable during the construction of Tillamook Station, servicing other lighthouses on the west coast. However, she happened to be in Astoria during early June, 1880, and came to the rescue of a delayed delivery schedule. The *George Harley*, which had been chartered for hauling the ashlar rock to the construction site, and was due at Astoria by June 4, had been delayed. The *Schubrick's* Captain made his ship available, and hauled enough stone, brick, cement, and other materials to the Rock to enable the corner stone of the lighthouse to be laid on June 22, 1880.

In August, the masonry work on the Rock was progressing faster than stone could be delivered. To speed up the availability of materials, and to take advantage of good weather, the small schooner *Emily Stephens* was chartered to haul 500 tons of building materials, at a rate of $10 per ton. A hoisting apparatus was rigged on her deck and powered by a steam donkey. The *Stephens* had a square stern and was a schooner-rigged sailing vessel of only 68 tons, but she proved to be a very productive workhorse.

Because of ever changing weather conditions, summer fogs, drenching rains and winter storms, the positioning and construction of the lighthouse were given great scrutiny. The dwelling and the tower had to be built to the demanding specifications given to the masons by Mr. Gillespie, the Lighthouse Engineer.

The consideration of where the light beacon would be positioned, above the sea, was determined by what was to be the station's lowest safe distance above the water, 90 feet. This established the level of the beacon at 136 feet, to make the light visible from sea even though the headland behind it might be engulfed in fog.

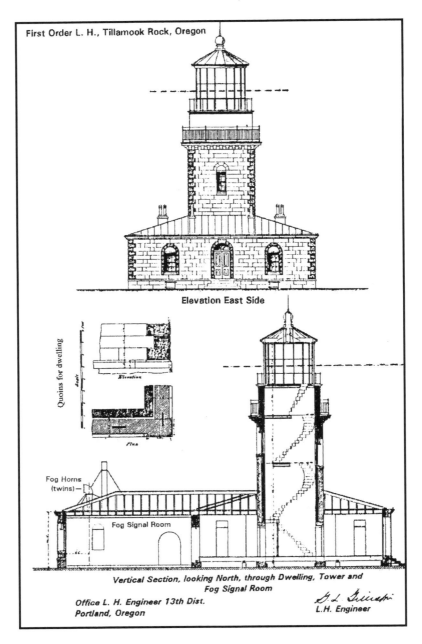

First Order L. H., Tillamook Rock, Oregon

Elevation East Side

Quoins for dwelling

Elevation

Plan

Fog Horns
(twins)

Fog Signal Room

*Vertical Section, looking North, through Dwelling, Tower and
Fog Signal Room*

Office L. H. Engineer 13th Dist.
Portland, Oregon

L.H. Engineer

The initial measurements of the Rock, made by Mr. Wheeler, were found to be surprisingly correct and indicated that, at a 90 foot level, the building envelope would give the structure a platform of 80 by 45 feet. With this space available, a building was designed that would provide comfortable quarters for four lighthouse Keepers, as well as ample storage for up to six months of food and fuel. This dwelling was built of the quarried stone, one story high, 48 by 45, plus an extension on the west side for the fog signal room, which is 32 by 28 feet, all under the same roof. The original plan elevation shows a hip roof line. This style of roof was discarded in favor of a single flat roof, for better rain-water collection.

The light, which was timed to show one white flash every five seconds, was exhibited from the stone tower extending from the center of the main structure. This tower is 16 feet square. The walls of the tower are the same thickness as the walls of the dwelling (16 inches), and enclose a circular staircase. The tower height is 35 feet, 6 inches above the foundation, and is finished with a brick parapet upon which rests the light lantern.

Note the size and shape of the windows on the Elevation Plan. Many have argued that the windows were portholes, not standard rectangular windows with ropes and sash-weights. But the drawings and the construction notes all indicate that the windows were the standard type, installed with safety glass. In actuality, both opinions are correct. The original windows were installed as shown on the plan. However, over the years, because of the many horrendous storms, some of the windows, especially on the windward side of the station, had to be replaced with portholes due to storm damage. These round brass windows had three-inch-thick glass and could be 'dogged down' and made watertight during the many storms.

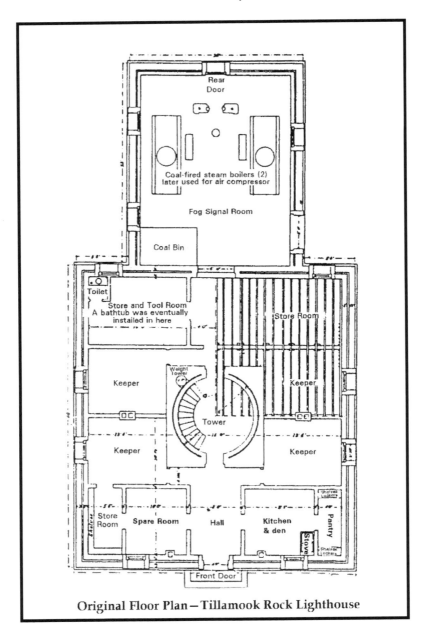

Original Floor Plan—Tillamook Rock Lighthouse

The exterior walls were 16 inches thick and made of ashlar stone. The interior walls were 8 inches thick and made from the same material. This type of stone is a finely dressed masonry that dates back to Inca and Aztec architecture. Around the perimeter of the main structure were a number of rooms. These included four sleeping rooms for the Keepers, positioned with two rooms on the north side and two on the south. Each room was 10 by 12 feet. From the front door, and off the 30 inch wide hallway, are four more rooms: the kitchen and pantry on one side of the hall, and a room designated as a 'spare' plus a storeroom, on the other side of the hall. The 'spare' room was generally used as a parlor and for food storage. At the back of the building was a 'storage and tool room' off of which, in a corner, was an enclosed toilet. Another storeroom occupied the remainder of the building except for the tower, which was in the center and ran from the base of the floor up through the roof. The hall, from the front door on the east side of the building, went completely through the building, including the base of the tower to the fog signal room. The two boilers for supplying steam to the fog horns were arranged parallel to the north and south walls of the room. These boilers were 15 feet apart with the engines placed between them. One engine worked the right boiler and the other the left. The fire boxes opened toward the Keeper's dwelling and provided the only heat for the station. These boilers were 6 feet 6 inches from the west wall so the tubes could be readily cleaned or replaced. The smoke pipes passed into a low brick chimney that was positioned between the outer ends of the boilers, which were topped with a sheet-iron hood surmounted by the 16 foot iron smoke stack. (Over the years, this smoke stack was constantly damaged by the many storms.) The horn trumpets were positioned in front of the smoke stack and passed vertically through the roof then curved 90 degrees and pointed westward with bell shaped openings for the best transmission of sound. The blasts lasted five seconds at intervals of one minute. The horns and the boilers were cross connected so either siren could be operated with either boiler.

These boilers required a great amount of water so rain was collected from the roof of the station and carried to a brick lined cistern which was excavated out of the solid rock on the north side. The cistern had a capacity of 13,000 gallons. When the fog horns were working, at a pressure of 72 pounds of steam, the water consumed was 130 gallons each hour. During the first summer of operation, the fog signals worked 65 hours and consumed nearly 9000 gallons of water. This cistern system was essential to the operation of the station, and rain was a valuable commodity.

These plans also reveal the lack of creature comforts for the Keepers. There was a kitchen, with a coal-fired cook stove, but no icebox or sink is shown. The kitchen is also called the den. This room is where the men socialized and worked out the duties of running and maintaining the station. No central heating, laundry or bathing facilities were noted. With winds howling and a drenching rain, one can only imagine the ripe kitchen on Saturday nights. Four hefty Keepers, dressed only in their long johns, would share a copper tub of hot water in the lantern light, washing off the sweat and grime of a full week's work.

The plan also notes a toilet in the tool and storage room. One of the first things built on the Rock was a small stone outhouse that opened to the sea below. This facility worked just fine in calm seas. During stormy weather, however, the updraft from the pounding surf below was so violent that sea-water, pebbles and waste would pellet the underside of the toilet seat. This 'reverse flow' privy became the hazing symbol for all the new Keepers to the Rock. They were told that the stone outhouse was the *only* facility on the station and that it shouldn't be used when the seas were stormy. Not the best news for green-gilled newcomers!

Early Photo of
Completed Lighthouse
Looking SSW

Fresnel Light

Storage Tanks

Rock Fissure

Tramway

Cargo Landing Area

Fog Horn Trumpets

Brick Chimney

Old Outhouse

Motor Room

Derrick

© Brian D. Ratty

Graphic: Brian D. Ratty

Most of the specifications used for the construction of the station were from the earliest reports by Mr. Gillespie, the Lighthouse Engineer. Over the years, many remodeling and modernization projects accounted for substantial changes. At the time of the original construction, there was no mention of any electrical needs or any means of communications with the mainland. The lighthouse was totally isolated from the outside world, depending solely on food, oil lanterns, coal and water for its daily operations. All of these, including the drinking water, had to be supplied via ships whose schedules were erratic because of the weather. It would be many years before electrification, air compressors, diesel powered generators and undersea phone lines would be installed. Being a lighthouse Keeper, marooned on the Rock, was a rigorous life only fit for the hardiest souls.

Photo: CCHS, Astoria, Oregon

Remodeled Station About 1920

Chapter Five

Light and Horns

Fresnel lenses have been used in the production of motion pictures, by still photographers, and in lighthouse towers ever since the concept was first invented by French physicist Augustin Fresnel in 1822. The first order Fresnel lens for lighthouses was made in France and shipped to the United States, starting in the mid-19th Century. Each lens consists of concentric rings of glass prisms that bend the light coming from a lamp inside the lens into a narrow beam. This lens has 1,176 prisms and 24 bulls-eyes. At the center, the bulls-eyes work as a magnifying glass so that the light beam is more powerful. The lens sections are held together by brass frames weighing five tons. The entire lens weighs in at approximately seven tons.

This type of lens can throw a beam of light to a distance of 22 miles. Tests showed that an open flame lantern lost nearly 97% of its light, and that a flamed lantern with reflectors behind it lost 83% of its light. The Fresnel lens was able to capture all but 17% of its light.

At first, an oil lamp with five wicks provided the light source. Kerosene was the preferred fuel. With the advent of electricity, lamps came into use.

There were many different grades of Fresnel lenses for lighthouses. The first order lens was considered the best, with the longest reach, and was coveted by most light stations. The first order lantern used at the Tillamook Lighthouse was by far the single most expensive item on the Rock.

First Order Fresnel Lens

A winding-type clock mechanism caused the Fresnel lens to revolve, and was an ingenious mechanical solution in the age before electric power. A weight – like the weights in a grandfather clock – dropped 17 feet through a shaft called the channel of the lighthouse tower. This channel extended from under the floor of the lantern room down to the first floor. The weight powered a clock in the lantern room that regulated the rotation and blinking of the lens. It took 7½ hours for the weight to complete its descent. The Keeper would climb into the tower to rewind the clock by using a hand crank to pull the weight back up to the top of the channel, to start a new descent and keep the light operating.

The Tillamook light beacon was electrified in 1924, when the fuel source was changed from an oil vapor lamp to a 300-watt electric lamp. The living quarters were not electrified until 1932, when steam heating was also installed. Before that, the Keepers used kerosene lamps for light at night.

In April of 1880, the Lighthouse Board contracted with a San Francisco company for $8,200 to provide a first order Fresnel lantern and the necessary metal work. During construction, some of the needed metal work arrived in July of 1881. This included the clock mechanism that allowed the lens to turn and blink during normal operations. The last sections of the lens, together with the lantern, were delivered in September of 1880. For some unexplained reason, this equipment did not include wicks and mirrors for the main tower lantern. This delay would soon have tragic consequences.

In June of 1880, a requisition was made for duplicate fog sirens of the first class. The order included boilers to generate steam, and allied machinery. The theory was that these could be produced at a lower cost on the east coast by firms that held patents on such equipment and who had experience with similar work. The New York contractor would manufacture all equipment specified, and box it for delivery to the Depot Quartermaster in New York City. The cost was $5,100. The quartermaster received the apparatus on December 1, 1880, for shipment to Portland, and it reached there on January 13, 1881. The contract was awarded to a vender that had experience manufacturing locomotive-type boilers that could provide enough steam for the sirens. The boilermaker was also required to supply all necessary fittings, do the testing of the horns in Portland, and demonstrate that the entire system was in good running order before being shipped to the job site.

One can only imagine the response of neighboring Portlanders while the testing of these 'steam-horns' was in process. After all of the necessary inspections were completed, the apparatus was repackaged and shipped on a riverboat to the wharf in Astoria. The boilermaker received $3,550 for its work.

The fog signals were finally delivered to the light-house, where the apparatus was immediately set in place. Upon further inspection, however, the installation crew noticed that both sirens had been damaged while being transported from Portland. Replacement horns were ordered that delayed fog-signal operations from February 8, 1881 to March 4, 1881. This note of readiness was first printed in the "Notice to Mariners" bulletins for that date. This delay of the fog signals would soon have tragic consequences, as well.

The slightly smaller steam schooner *George Harley* made its first trip to the Rock in June of 1880. This was the ship fitted as a "wrecker," with its large steam driven derrick. The *Harley* was equipped with a powerful engine that could make five knots in still water. The boats Skipper was known for his good judgment and great energy, and for the crews capacity for hard work, as well as their ability to land supplies with great efficiency. The ship did not lose a single item or break a single article entrusted to it during the construction.

With workers coming and going, and supplies arriving every few weeks, the construction continued through the summer, into the fall, and then into the unforgiving winter months. As the station took shape, concerns about food, fuel and drinking water took center stage. A coal bin was built on the south side of the fog signal room, where hundreds of gunny sacks of coal were stored for the boilers and cook stove. Next came hundreds of gallons of kerosene for the Fresnel lamp and the station's many hand lanterns. Drinking water arrived in sealed wooded barrels that filled the storage rooms from floor to ceiling. Finally, the food supplies were delivered on wooden pallets and in wooden boxes of all descriptions and sizes. Every item was logged in and placed exactly as planned, totaling enough pro-visions for the lighthouse to survive for a half-year without resupply.

The Tillamook Rock light was different in many ways from the other lighthouses operating on the west coast. The station's biggest shortcoming was its location on a small rock island, one mile off-shore, with no way of leaving the island during emergencies. Other than signal flags, which were seldom if ever used, there was absolutely no communication with shore. If the lighthouse needed help or supplies, those could only come by ship, weather permitting. The station didn't even have its own surfboat, when operations started in early 1881. Like monks in a monastery everyone on the island, whether work crews or Keepers, were totally isolated and on their own. This isolation would make the Tillamook Rock Lighthouse the loneliest station in the lighthouse service.

With each stone and brick in place, and with each storage tank and room filled with food and fuel, the lighthouse neared completion, and plans were made for a gala celebration of lighting the light. The first four lighthouse Keepers were scheduled to arrive on January 20, 1881. The hand carved headstone over the front door was put in place with the inscription: *Tillamook Rock L.H. - December of 1880*. All seemed ready for the festivities. The work was almost done; soon, the light would illumine the night sky, and the horns of warning would be heard. But then the weather blew in a tragic mystery ship which dashed any hopes of a lighting celebration.

At midnight on January 21, 1881, without fanfare, and with no official ceremony, the five wicks of the oil lamp were lit, and the mechanism for turning the light was started. The night sky around the rock came alive with a narrow beam of light that flashed every five seconds and could be seen 22 miles out to sea.

When finished, the lighthouse stood 90 feet above the ocean, with a 36 foot brick tower rising out of the middle of the main structure, atop stood a ten-foot-tall lantern room. Attached to the main castle-like lighthouse, on the west side, was the one story fog signal room, with trumpets facing due west. This island and lighthouse would soon prove to be the nastiest chunk of rubble anywhere in the world.

The first landing on Tillamook Rock had been on June of 1879. The first overnight stay on the island happened in October of 1879. In May of 1880, the top of the rock had been decapitated by removing 29 feet of rubble. The corner stone of the station had been set in June of 1880, and by January of 1881 the buildings were completed, including the installation of the first order Fresnel lens. In March of 1881, the fog signal operations were working.

After 575 days of planning and construction, the Tillamook Rock light began her 77 year long career of standing guard at the south entrance to the Columbia River Bar and keeping the sea lanes open. The total cost of building the Tillamook Rock Lighthouse was one life and $123,492.82. The incident with the mystery ship would sadly add another 14 lives to that list.

Shipwrecks

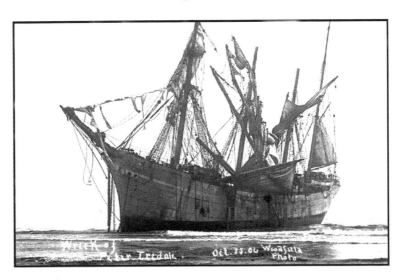

Two British shipwrecks
Top Peter Iredale 1906 Bottom Glenesslin 1913

Chapter Six

The Mystery Ship

No story about the Tillamook Rock Lighthouse would be complete without including this tragic tale. This is the author's adaptation of the real-life story of the British ship Lupatia.

A violent gust of wind riddled the glass of the kitchen's only window. At the same time, the room quivered with the pounding of the surf.

"What the hell was that?" the wide-eyed 22 year old apprentice mason asked, eating his dinner of beans and bacon.

"It's just the wind, Nathan," his father across the table answered.

"I could swear I heard a dog bark," the young man said, looking up at his four other tablemates.

The Construction Superintendent, Mr. Wheeler, chuckled. "No dogs out here, son. Only rain and wind."

On the stormy north Oregon coast, some twenty miles south of the Columbia River Bar, lies the formidable promontory of Sitka Spruce called Tillamook Head. This headland of steep, rocky bluffs rises up over twelve hundred feet at its peak, with an unobstructed view of the Pacific Ocean. Just one mile off shore of this Head is an isolated basaltic rock of less than one acre, where hardy visionaries and skilled craftsmen had toiled for 560 days to build the Tillamook Rock Lighthouse.

Three days before, on New Year's Day of 1881, a terrible tempest had rolled over the new lighthouse with gale force winds and drenching rains. The weather had not let up for seventy-two straight hours. The skeleton crew of workers had taken refuge inside the new station to finish a short list of construction details that still needed tending.

"I think the boy is coming down with rock fever," Gill Gibbons, the pug-faced Master Mason, said, looking at his son. "He's hearing things in the wind."

Nathan was a tall, lean, good-looking lad who had learned long ago how to deal with his father. "Unlike some, I've got young ears and I know a dog's bark."

Captain Wheeler, as the men called the Superintendent, poured himself some more coffee. He was a fine-looking middle-aged man with a salt-and-pepper widows peak and a friendly face with an eye for detail and a passion for getting the job done. He was the big boss of everything and everybody on the Rock.

"Gill, when will you be done with the stone floors?" he asked, adding sugar to his brew.

The mason looked up from his plate. "A few more days inside and a few more outside, if the weather improves."

Just then, the door opened and Albert Hook, the Boilermaker, entered the small, warm kitchen, carrying an unlit storm lantern. He was a tall, lean man with a dark pencil mustache, wearing a blue wool coat that was wet from the rain.

"Did you find that part you needed?" the Captain asked.

Albert took off his coat and placed it on the back of his chair. "Yep, right there in the tool shed."

"When will the boilers be ready?" the Captain asked, watching him move to the stove for his dinner.

Albert filled his plate and turned back to the table. "The boilers are almost done, but we won't have the new horns until the next supply ship."

Another gust of wind swirled around the station, with the surf exploding against the base of the monolith.

The Captain frowned. "We need our fog horns on days like these. Bud, how are you doing with the new light?"

Bud Larson, the pale-skinned Beacon Mechanic, had just finished installing the first-order Fresnel lens atop the tower. He was now finishing with the clockwork mechanism that would turn the light during operations.

"All I'm waiting for is the wicks and mirrors, and we'll be ready to light it up."

The Captain shook his head and stood from the table. "I feel helpless out here without a light or horns."

"Is the weather letting up any?" Nathan asked the boilermaker.

"The rain has some, but now there's a fog low on the water."

"It's getting dark," the Captain said, drinking the last of his coffee. "I'll go have a look around outside."

"Better take a storm lantern, Captain. It gets damn dark out here so fast," Albert said, handing him the unlit light.

"I'll come with you," Nathan added, getting to his feet. "Let me get the binoculars. Maybe I'll see that dog I heard."

His father snickered. "It be a waste of time, son. There ain't nothing out there but the voice of God." Gill Gibbons was a fireplug of a man, with arms as thick as his thighs, and a complexion as rough as the stones he laid. He was an old-time craftsman who worked for pride and price, while his son Nathan thought laying bricks wasn't a worthwhile enterprise.

Proudly, Gill had personally overseen the placement of every stone and brick during the building of the lighthouse. And, along the way, he had taught his son the many tricks to the trade: 'level plumb and square - measure twice, score and cut once – if you can't do it right, don't do it at all.' His father's words were like the Gospel, and both men lived by them.

After the Captain and Nathan were gone, Sam Wyatt, the Painter, looked up from his meal and asked, through a mouthful of beans, "What the hell are they looking for? I didn't hear nothin'."

Albert glared back at him. The painter had a permanent scowl on his face and was notorious for his negative thinking and constant complaining.

"Sea nymphs Sam," the boilermaker answered. "They often come out when the fog hugs the water. They're quite a sight to see. You might want to join them."

He smirked at his tablemates and continued stuffing his face. Sam Wyatt was a strange little man, devoid of a sense of humor or personality. But he was one hell of a good painter.

The lighthouse was perched on a large basaltic rock, 90 feet above the boiling sea. The main building and tower were constructed entirely of brick and stone, and the lantern room with its new light was a 135 feet above the ocean. The front door of the station faced due east, looking out at the distant shore, while the backdoor was at the end of the fog signal room, looking due west to the Pacific Ocean. From a mariner's point of view, this white castle-like structure seemed like an impregnable bastion of safety.

On the front porch, the men were greeted by a murky fading twilight, with churning green seas as far as the eye could see. The rain had stopped, but the wind and fog still swirled around the station like a whirlwind. With the limited visibility, they quickly walked around the outside of the building to the back door. There, in the fleeting sunlit, they saw only endless acres of gray. But then Nathan heard muffled voices traveling on the wind, and the bark of a dog again. Quickly, he turned his binoculars to the southwest.

"Did you hear that, Captain?" he shouted over the sounds of the pounding surf.

"Yes!" he answered quickly. "And I caught a glimpse of a ship's red light – 600 yards out, south-southwest."

Nathan handed him the glasses. "They seem to be coming right at us. What do we do?"

With the binoculars to his eyes, the Captain replied, "I see two of her masts above the fog. Yes, she's heading our way."

"How do we stop her?" Nathan asked in a panic.

"A big bonfire will get her attention," the Captain answered calmly. "Let's go inside and get the crew."

The two men burst in through the kitchen door like a hurricane. The Captain rattled off what they had seen and heard, and started giving orders like an Army General.

"Gill, you take the men and collect two lanterns each. Get them lit, take them up into the tower, and stand outside on the catwalk, waving the lamps so the ship might see you. Nathan and I will collect some empty food crates and get a bonfire going on the lip of the rock. Move it, guys! We don't have much time."

Everyone scattered instantly to their assignments. The Captain and Nathan rushed into the storerooms to gather wooden boxes, then made one last stop, to the Head Keeper's bedroom, where they grabbed a voice horn and a can of kerosene before rushing out the back door and into the weather again.

With the speed of a wrecking ball, Nathan dismantled the crates with brute force, then ran back inside the station for more boxes. The Captain drenched the wood with the kerosene and used his lit lantern to ignite the fire. As the flames took hold in the swirling winds, he looked up at the murky tower to see three of his crew waving lanterns in the evening sky. The Captain picked up the voice horn and started shouting, "Do not approach! Come about now! Rocks!"

The only answer was the wind.

Gill yelled from the tower, "We can see her red light. She's just southwest of us."

Nathan returned with more empty boxes and quickly began tearing them apart. He tossed the dry wood onto the fire, it shot up pillars of orange flames and sparks that grew to over 20 feet in height. The firelight lit up the side of the lighthouse, and the men on the catwalk continued shouting warnings while frantically waving their lanterns. Just as the Superintendent was about to use the voice horn again, they all clearly heard the voice of the ship's Captain shouting, "Coming about," and then the bark of a dog. The men could also plainly hear the creaking of the ship's timbers, and flapping of the sails as the ship turned away.

"Which way is she turning?" the Captain yelled up to the men in the tower.

"Can't see her light no more. Think she turned for open water," Gill shouted over the wind, as the men on the catwalk let out a loud roar of approval.

The Captain glanced skyward and gave them the thumbs up, with a smile. Then he put his hand on Nathan's shoulder. "How's it feel to save some lives, son?"

The young man just stood there for the longest moment, staring at the fire. He had finally found a worthwhile enterprise, and it felt so damn good!

The Captain shouted up to his men, "Get out of the weather. I'll see you inside."

When the Superintendent walked into the kitchen, he carried something seldom seen on a lighthouse: a bottle of whiskey. He looked around at his beleaguered crew, who were all cold and disheveled from the weather.

"I got this on my last shore leave, and you boys sure earned some, tonight." He poured two fingers of whiskey into each man's coffee mug…except for Sam Wyatt, the painter. He had remained in the warm kitchen during the entire incident. His excuse was that he hadn't believed there was anything out there.

Holding his coffee mug high, the Captain made a toast. "Here's to the Skipper and crew of the Mystery Ship. May she find a safe port and live a long life."

The men celebrated their life-saving actions until the bottle was dry.

British Bark Lupatia

That night, the construction crew had no way of knowing that they had just saved the 1,300 ton British ship *Lupatia*. She was a square-rigged brigantine, bound for Portland after making the long crossing from Japan. The ship's company had lost their Captain early in the voyage, and command had fallen to the ship's mate (and younger brother) of the deceased Captain. The *Lupatia* was under ballast and making her way north to the mouth of the Columbia River while hugging the coast. With a strong south-westerly wind and a heavy fog, and maybe a malfunctioning compass, the new Skipper had become confused and lost his way.

At first light the next morning, Nathan got out of bed and dressed quickly. When he got to the kitchen, he found the Captain just lighting the coal-stove.

"Why are you up so early?"

Nathan slipped on his jacket and grabbed the binoculars. "I fussed all night about that damn ship we saved. I have to go see for myself."

The Captain nodded. "I'll join you, after I get the coffee on."

At first, when he stepped out onto the sunny front stoop, everything looked normal. The sea was as smooth as molasses, with gentle green swells and unlimited visibility. Then his heart sank like a brick. The water around the island was full of floating rubbish. He saw parts of a shattered topmast and other portions of rigging bobbing in the water. There were also hatch covers and wooden planks torn apart like match sticks. He put the binoculars to his eyes, with his head reeling. He looked towards Tillamook Head, and then slowly panned the glasses down the shoreline. Just south of Bird Point, he found the woeful source of the debris: the flotsam of a ship scattered among the rocks where it had likely broken apart in the storm. Then he looked farther south to Indian Beach, where he saw some figures walking the sands, but they were too far away to see clearly.

Nathan lowered the binoculars, with tears in eyes. "We didn't save a damn thing!" he said out loud. That's when he realized the Captain was standing right next to him. Without a word, he handed him the glasses.

"We should have done more."

"Like what?" the Captain replied, looking through the binoculars.

"Thrown some sticks of dynamite over the cliff so they would have seen us sooner."

"The wind would have blown them back on the station," he answered calmly.

"We could have tried the signal flags."

The Captain lowered his glasses. "At night? Look, son, without light and horns, any lighthouse can only be a witness to tragedy."

"I feel like we let them down. What now?"

The Captain's sad blue eyes regarded the young man. "There will be a search for any survivors, and a Board of Inquiry will be convened. In a few weeks or months, we will know what happened to our Mystery Ship. In the meantime, you should consider joining the Lighthouse Service. You've got the right grit for it, and you would make a terrific Keeper of the light."

Nathan thought a moment, looking out at the floating debris. "Sounds like a worthwhile enterprise to me, Captain."

Daylight dashed any hopes that the ship had escaped. On the shore, that morning, the bodies of 12 men were revealed, washed up on the beach. Four members of the 16 person crew were never found. All of the recovered bodies were buried in a large common grave with a tombstone of wreckage from the ship. But there was one survivor. The searchers found the ship's half-grown Australian Shepherd dog whimpering around the bodies on that morning. He had a belly full of seawater, and was near death after swimming more than a mile through the frigid waters to the shore. He could not tell the story of his lost companions. But that night, in the lighthouse kitchen, Nathan swore he could still hear a dog howling.

The accident of the *Lupatia* weighed heavily on the minds of the Tillamook workers, who could not help but wonder if things might have turned out differently had the lighthouse been operational. One of them later remarked, "From that hour on, finishing the station to get the light lit and the foghorn going was more than just a job." The tower was finally lit just 19 days later, on January 21, 1881. The fog horn didn't start operating until March, another sad mark to tarnish the reputation of Terrible Tilly.

Ode to the Ship *Lupatia*
by James A. Gibbs

Why did you fail, O ship of sail,
There mangled on the reef?
Why did you fain the bounding main –
For now you've come to grief.

No hope in sight all through the night,
The dismal, abysmal dark –
You missed the light, O what a sight,
You came far short of the mark.

In too far, short of the bar,
The human hand has failed,
Rudder bent, wheel is rent;
To rock and sand you're nailed.

No route to ply, 'tis here you die,
Your coffin closed so tight –
No more to roam through ocean foam,
Your crew has lost the fight.

Why did you fail, O ship of sail –
Your bones to bleach in brine,
No star-filled sky to steer you by,
No gravestone – no hope – no shrine

Chapter Seven

Not an Ordinary Job

After the end of the American Civil War in 1865, the country started tiptoeing into the Gilded Age of the Industrial Revolution. By the time the Transcontinental Railroad was completed in 1869, America stood on the brink of becoming an International world power, largely due to all of her vast natural resources. To achieve this status, however, safe maritime commerce would have to be established. What America needed was a transportation network like no other in the world. While the 'iron highway' would link the eastern seaboard to the west and the Gulf States to the north, it would be a system of lighthouses and other navigational aids that would link the coastal and inland ports together into a large, safe network of maritime commerce.

The Lighthouse Board, originally created in 1789, operated under the Department of the Treasury. The United States Lighthouse Service or the Bureau of Lighthouses (USLHS) was created in 1852. This Government agency hired all types of personnel, including administrative, engineering, maintenance, light Keepers, a small navy of ships (lighthouse tenders), and hundreds of seamen to build, maintain and operate lighthouses. Also at this time, the placement of aids to navigation along rivers had become the responsibility of the Lighthouse Service, and many of these aids were tended on a part-time basis by local citizens called Lamp Lighters or Lamp Attendants.

The Lighthouse Board was a Federal bureaucracy employing thousands of people, with reams of rules and regulations.

A lighthouse Keeper was the person responsible for tending and caring for a lighthouse, particularly the light and lens in the days when oil lamps and clockwork mechanisms were used. Lighthouse Keepers were some-times referred to as "wickies" because of their job trimming the wicks.

Lives depended on the light Keepers. Their duties were vast and varied, and the Keepers depended on the 1881 Employee Instruction Manual. The following is an excerpt from that manual:

Lights must be exhibited punctually at sunset and kept lighted at full intensity until sunrise, when the lights will be extinguished and the apparatus put in order without delay for relighting.

Preparations for lighting the beacon began well before dusk. The Keeper first inspected the Fresnel lens and its many prisms, which were cleaned that morning. The lamp that produced the light was checked and the supply of fuel refilled. The wick was trimmed and lighted. The weights, which dropped down the tower shaft driving gears that caused the lens to revolve, were unlocked, hand cranked up to the top and a new descent started.

At stations having one or more assistant Keepers, watches must be kept and so divided. At stations having no assistant, the Keeper must not leave the light for at least half an hour after lighting, in order to see that it is burning properly, and must visit the light at least twice between 8 p.m. and sunrise, and on stormy nights must be constantly looked after.

When not in the lighthouse, the Keeper would spend some time everyday outside surveying weather and tide conditions and taking readings. Where installed and under the Keeper's command, buoys and markers would be checked and repositioned as needed. If there was a launch, lifeboat or any other vessel assigned to the station, it too was checked.

In addition to tending the light, the Keeper's routine duties included: cleaning the tower and living quarters daily, painting as needed, making repairs, fixing the machinery as needed, installing any replacement equipment, conducting tours of the lighthouse for USLHS Inspectors and Engineers during quarterly inspections, maintaining the grounds, and planting and tending a personal vegetable garden. This final regulation would be hard to follow on Tillamook Rock!

As with most Government bureaucracies, there was a hierarchy with the light Keepers. The Head Keeper was in charge of everything at the station. He, and on a rare occasion she, was the boss and the primary supervisor. The Head Keeper had assistant Keepers, from first assistant to fourth. Small stations might have only one assistant, while large lighthouses such as Tillamook Rock had up to four assistants on station.

All personnel involved with lighthouses were members of The United States Lighthouse Service, and were paid as civil servants. Unlike the military, the Service allowed for the recruitment of both men and women as lighthouse Keepers, although most women were part of a family unit that ran specific light stations. In 1881, a Head Keeper would be paid approximately $60 month, while lower-grade Keepers were paid anywhere from $25 to $45 per month. This pay was in addition to all costs of food and shelter paid for by the Government, but did not include any allotment for clothing. Their work duties included working three months per tour of duty, seven days a week, and ten to twelve hours per day. After such a tour, they received a paid shore leave of two weeks, without any appropriations for upkeep.

Uniforms were introduced in 1883. USLHS believed that the uniforms worn by all of its 1,600 members would help maintain discipline and increase efficiency. Most of the time, personnel at land based stations, off shore lights and USLHS vessels wore work uniforms consisting of dungaree blouses and trousers or overalls, and conical, flat-top navy blue caps. On work detail, black or tan shoes could be worn with black socks. When at USLHS functions or in public, when representing the Service, Keepers and other personnel were required to wear the dress uniform, which was the same as a U.S. Navy Officers uniform but with USLHS markings. Women Keepers were exempt from the uniform regulations. Male Keepers had to buy their own uniforms.

Photo: CRMM, Astoria, Oregon
Keepers took turns cooking. This Keeper is making donuts
in the Tillamook station kitchen in 1920.

A *lighthouse tender* is a ship specifically designed to maintain, support, or tend to lighthouses or light vessels, delivering supplies, fuel, and mail, and providing transportation. In the United States, these ships originally served as part of the Lighthouse Service, and now are part of the US Coast Guard. The first American tender of the

Lighthouse Service was a former revenue cutter *Rush*, which was acquired in 1840. The first steam tender was the *Shubrick*, completed in 1857 and put into service on the west coast in 1858. The *Fir* was the last active representative of the service, and is now a U.S. National Historic Landmark. Lighthouse tenders also towed lightships to stations (prior to powered light vessels) and transferred the Keepers, their families and possessions from station to station. The tender was the vehicle used by the District Inspector for his yearly white-glove inspection of all light stations.

Revenue Cutter Rush

With the arrival of the first Head Keeper, Albert Roeder, and three assistants, the Fresnel lens on the Tillamook Rock Lighthouse was lit on January 21, 1881. Unfortunately, Mr. Roeder would be the first of four Head Keepers stationed on the Rock during the first two years of its operation. Finding and retaining light Keepers for the Tillamook Rock Lighthouse would be a continual challenge for the USLHS.

Two hundred and one days after the laying of the corner stone, the lighthouse was operational. The largest single cost for building the station was $26,391.91 for transportation to and from Tillamook Rock; this figure included the rental of all ships and crews. The next most expensive item was $9,463.20 for the ashlar stone, which was quarried from Mount Tabor in Portland, Oregon. The most expensive single item brought to the Rock was the Fresnel lens and the related mechanical work for $8,200.00. The total cost of construction at $123,492.82 was more than the Lighthouse Board had originally estimated but, thanks to Mr. Wheeler, Superintendent of Construction, and Mr. Ballantyne, the Foreman, the finished lighthouse was considered an engineering marvel. At the time, no one at the Lighthouse Board or the District offices realized the magnitude of the challenges facing Tilly.

The light station was 30 miles from the nearest harbor, and was located off a dangerous, rocky portion of the north Oregon coast, difficult to reach even in a quiet sea. No approach could be made during a storm of even the most minor nature. There was no mainland road within 20 miles, and no emergency beach landing point for nearly half of that distance. The Tillamook Rock Lighthouse was one of the most isolated stations in the world. Therefore, it was necessary for the Lighthouse Service to maintain a chartered ship that could master the rough sea outside the Columbia River Bar. Some funds could have been saved by discharging this vessel after the major part of the construction was completed, but to do so, it would have placed all the men, still on the Rock, in potential jeopardy in the event of an emergency evacuation, or if an accident occurred.

There was excellent cooperation from all of the steamship companies whose ship Captains had taken an interest in the project from the very beginning. The foreman on the job site was equipped with a set of International code flags, and ships passing the Rock in either direction stood in close to read the flags for messages that might call for assistance.

On two occasions, when fog was thick and visibility limited, the foreman made known the location of the Rock to approaching ships by exploding giant powder cartridges over the sea in the direction of the approaching ships bell. It was not determined whether these signals prevented disasters, but effectively these small signal flags were one of the only means of communications between the lighthouse and the outside world.

The new beacons importance to maritime commerce was considered to be great. A suggestion was made to the Government that the station be connected with Point Adams Lighthouse or with Cape Disappointment Lighthouse by telegraph. Light House Engineer, Mr. Glimpse wrote:

At an early day an attempt will be made to have the general government extend the area of its usefulness by connecting it with the mainland either to Point Adams or to Cape Disappointment by a telegraph line in order to give ship owners early notice of the approach of expected steamers and vessels and likewise to inform their captains of the state of the bar at the entrance to the Columbia River. When this improvement has been added it is believed that the station will then be completed in every particular.

By this time, the telegraph was common throughout the country but telephones did not come into the engineers thinking because this was a new invention that was not yet widely appreciated. Many years later, an undersea cable carrying a telephone line from Tillamook Rock to the shore on Indian Beach at Ecola State Park was installed. The line was out-of-order, according to reports, as often as it was working, due to damage by storms.

The construction to the lighthouse was done, but not complete. In the spring of 1881, workers returned to the island with a long list of improvements to be made.

Swing Bridge

Great thought was given to developing a swinging bridge to replace the discomfort and danger of the breeches buoy for personnel visiting or leaving the station. The swinging bridge could be used to reach a boat within a distance of 30 feet from the Rock. This was a wrought iron movable bridge revolving around a vertical axis, similar to a railroad turntable. One arm was 35 feet long, and the opposite arm was 10 feet long, with a counterbalance on the shorter end. The bridge was on the edge of the Rock's northeast slope, near the 15 foot level, on a bench excavated expressly for it. The bridge was moved by hand, with geared wheels. When the bridge swung outwards, as to a visiting vessel, a descending rope ladder attached to the outer end enabled ascent. When the bridge was at rest, it was lashed to large ring bolts secured in the Rock to prevent damage during storms.

Early Sketch of Swing Bridge

This early sketch is believed to be the only illustration showing the proposed 35 foot-long "gangplank" on the lower edge of rock (A). The plan seemed reasonable, as the best way to land men and supplies from close-in ships, but apparently was never built. If it was, it was most likely washed into the sea by the next big storm to hit the Rock. Nothing on the Rock, not even the lightning rod atop the lantern house, was safe from being hit by the sea, as the entire place was 136 feet above the water and was sometimes totally under water during fierce winter storms.

Boat Ramp

Some references indicate that a tracked boat ramp was installed on the island. Iron rails for this ramp were secured deep into the Rock with lag bolts and cement. A wooden boat carriage would ride down these tracks and into the water, where a boat could be launched or retrieved. The light station was equipped with a standard New Bedford Whaleboat, and rigged with slings for launching and retrieval via a hand-cranked steel line on shore. The boat was kept in a small boat house underneath the supply house. This new ramp survived the first few months of operation, but then ferocious winter storms destroyed it. It was rebuilt the next summer, but then destroyed again. The idea of having a boat ramp was then abandoned, although the boat could still be launched by the derrick, which was a tricky operation.

New Bedford Whaleboat

In 1882, a few additional items were added to the station to complete it. These included railings, an exterior iron stairway, a coal and engine house, a tramway, a land-ing wharf, a bridge, and a retaining wall on the east side.

A new landing bridge was established in June of 1885 but was damaged by heavy surf that September. Although rebuilt by the following September, it would be destroyed again in December of the following year. The storm of December 1886 caused an unprecedented amount of dam-age. The following is an excerpt from the Annual Report of the Lighthouse Board:

In December, however, the heaviest surf known there broke over the station causing the damages as follows: The roofs on the south and west sides of the fog-signal room and on the west side of the dwelling were crushed in by the water and the part on the north side of the fog-signal room was displaced. The roof was loosened at the south side of the tower, allowing water to leak into the dwelling. The plastering in parts of the dwelling was jarred off and some was loosened by the water. The galvanized-iron chimney-tops were broken from two of the chimneys. The concrete covering of the top of the rock around the building was broken, and a brick parapet and concrete filling in a low place outside the fence at the southeast corner were carried away. A mass of the filling, weighing about half a ton, was thrown over the fence into the enclosure. Three 730-gallon water-tanks filled with water at the west end of the building were broken from their fastenings and piled against the fence. The ash-chute on the north side of the rock and the spar for swinging the derrick boom were broken away, but the latter was saved by one of its chain fastenings. The platform around the derrick was destroyed and some planks were broken from the landing platform. The landing bridge was carried away, having stood till nearly the end of the storm, when it failed, apparently by the breaking of the pivot at the bottom of which the mast rested.

What the Lighthouse Board soon determined, after building a lighthouse at such an exposed location, was that it was going to require continual maintenance. A storm in January of 1883 sent stones flying into the iron roof of the fog signal building, leaving twenty holes. The holes were temporarily repaired with putty, and soon replaced with galvanized sheet-iron.

In 1890, $6,000 was appropriated for a telegraph line to connect the station to Fort Stevens. Weather brought about many delays, over the years, adding to the workload of the lighthouse tender and requiring consent from land-owners, but communication was finally established on November 4, 1895.

The Keepers assigned to the lighthouse were a color-ful and diverse group. A typical days tour of duty began before dusk and continued well past dawn. The Keepers tended to a routine, but were always prepared to respond to any emergency, including shipwrecks.

Photo: CCHS, Astoria, Oregon

Rowing supplies to the Tillamook Rock Lighthouse

While the beacon was electrified in 1924, when the lens was changed from an oil vapor lamp to a 300-watt lamp, the living quarters were not electrified until 1932, when steam heating was also installed. Before that, the Keepers used kerosene lamps for light at night.

Keeper making log book entries

In 1897, a telephone line was installed however, a storm cut it shortly afterwards. During another storm in 1912, a hundred tons of rocks were reportedly shorn off the western end of the monolith, after that the windows were gradually cemented over, replaced by portholes.

Storms, damage, repair crews, and maintenance were constant visitors to the Tillamook Rock Lighthouse.

Chapter Eight
Decommissioning

The demise of manned lighthouses had many causes starting long before the actual closure of the stations. During World War I and immediately thereafter, several technological advances contributed to the automation of lighthouses, rendering human occupancy unnecessary. A device for automatically replacing burned-out electric lamps was developed and placed in several light stations in 1916. A bell alarm to warn Keepers of fluctuations in the burning efficiency of oil-vapor lamps was developed in 1917. In the same year, the first experimental wireless radios were installed in some select lighthouses.

Prior to the introduction of ship-to-shore radio, maritime communication was generally limited to line-of-sight visual signaling during clear weather, plus noise-makers such as bells and foghorns with only limited ranges. With the advent of wireless radio communications between ships and shore, maritime traffic could 'see' beyond the horizon, with a better understanding of approaching weather and sea conditions. Each major lighthouse soon became a radio and weather station, as well as a bright beacon in the night.

Technology wasn't the only reason for the downfall of the Tillamook Station. The many storms caused the USLHE to reflect on the high cost of maintenance and repairs. There were major gales in January of 1881 and 1883, and these tempests were only the beginning. A hurricane in December of 1886 swept away three wooden water tanks near the lighthouse, and sea water falling on the station, with the sound of a hundred hammers, crushed large sections of the roof and loosened plaster in the dwelling. A year later, a storm broke two panes of five-eighths-inch-thick glass and flooded the lantern room. First Assistant John Flynn was reportedly "floundering around in the lantern room like a sea lion after a salmon." To prevent further breakage of the glass panes during storms, a movable shield of strong wire that covered a quarter of the lantern room was sent to the Rock.

In the storm of December, 1894, this shield didn't prevent 13 panes of glass from being broken by a hurricane that tore fragments of rock loose and hurled them at the lantern room, damaging the lens and revolving apparatus. One monster piece of rubble, weighing nearly a ton, crashed through the roof of one of the men's rooms. At another point during the storm, there was six feet of water in the fog signal room and four feet in the living quarters. During a storm in 1896, a rock weighing 135 pounds crashed through the roof and into the kitchen of the Keeper's quarters. Storm waves frequently tossed rocks like bullets into the protective glass around the light's Fresnel lens.

During these storms, the custodians did not venture outside, as they feared they would be killed by flying debris that struck the station with the force of an explosive bomb. All that the Keepers could do was pray and "ride it out."

The only known death of a Keeper occurred on August 2, 1911, when Second Assistant Keeper Thomas Jones was painting the derrick and fell 35 feet onto rocks, sustaining terrible injuries. The steamer *Elmore* passed the station a few hours later, and offered to take Jones to the hospital at Bay City. Jones hung on for a period before passing away. On its way past Tillamook Rock the next week, the *Elmore* was once again hailed and asked to take off another Keeper. This time, fortunately, the injury was not life-threatening.

To deal with these many storms, the USLHE employed a large staff of maintenance engineers who traveled up and down the Oregon coast, repairing, replacing, and improving the coastal light stations. This crew was a constant visitor to the Tillamook Rock Lighthouse.

On October 21, 1934, the worst tempest ever recorded hit the lighthouse. The entire Pacific Northwest was inundated with a fierce and battering storm, and no one felt it more than the men trapped at Terrible Tilly. The sea spewed boulders through the lantern room ripping out iron bolts anchored three feet deep in the rock. Seawater flowed like a waterfall down the tower into the living quarters. The Lighthouse Service Bulletin carried the following account of the storm:

Repeatedly the entire station was completely submerged in tremendous seas which, meeting the precipitous side of the great rock, swept upward and over the masonry and ironwork structure surmounting the crest. A section of the rock itself was torn away, great fragments of it being thrown over the station, many of them through the plate glass of the first order lantern, 16 panels of which were shattered, rock fragments 60 pounds in weight falling inside. Unbroken seas flooded the lantern, filling the watch room, where the keepers struggled to erect storm shutters in the shattered lantern panels, submerged at times to their necks before the rush of water could escape through the door into the tower and quarters below. The inrushing seas brought fragments of rock and glass, and even small fish, with the flotsam. Assistant Keeper Hugo Hanson's hand was badly cut with flying glass.

The October 1934 storm destroyed the original Fresnel lens and leveled parts of the tower railing. Winds had reached 109 miles per hour, launching boulders and debris into the tower, damaging the lantern room and destroying the lens. The derrick and phone lines were destroyed, as well. After the storm subsided, communication with the lighthouse was severed until Keeper Henry Jenkins built a makeshift radio from the damaged foghorn and telephone parts to alert officials. Repairs to the lighthouse cost $12,000 and were not fully completed until February of 1935. The Fresnel lens was replaced by an aero beacon with a 17 mile reach, and a metal mesh was placed around the lantern room to protect the tower from large boulders.

In 1938, with war clouds on the horizon, President Roosevelt and his administration surveyed the Continental Coastal defenses for efficiencies in case of war. After the study, they ordered a coastal military reorganization, and established a plan to make lighthouse Keepers the eyes, ears, and first line of defense if war came. This new decree required extensive retraining, as well as the installation of up-to-date radio equipment for all manned lighthouses. The Keepers were now not only the masters of the light, the weathermen, and the radio operators, but also the unarmed first line of defense against any hostile foreign action. To protect the almost 600 lighthouses, in 32 states, the administration recommended the merger of the USLHE with the United States Coast Guard. This unification of the two services would provide armed protection for all U.S. lighthouses.

On July 1, 1939, the two oldest Government maritime services were combined. The USLHE had been under the Treasury Department, while the Coast Guard had been considered a bureau of the Department of Commerce. Officially, this merger was part of the President's Reorganization Plan #II, under the Reorganization Act of 1939. Under this Act, "the duties, responsibilities, and functions of the Commissioner of Lighthouses shall be vested in the Commandant of the Coast Guard," and all personnel of the Lighthouse Service were consolidated with the Coast Guard personnel. In many cases, Lighthouse Service personnel were given Coast Guard commissions, with ranks corresponding to their previous duties. No reduction in employment was made, and any such economy in personnel made possible through the merger was only the result of voluntary age retirements.

On July 7, 1939, the Bureau of Lighthouses, with all its equipment and staff, was moved to Coast Guard Headquarters in Washington DC. For convenience and expedition in the administration and operation of the enlarged Coast Guard, the former Coast Guard divisions and sections and the lighthouse districts were abolished and replaced by 13 districts, named in order as follows: Boston, New York, Norfolk, Jacksonville, New Orleans, San Juan, Cleveland, Chicago, St. Louis, San Francisco, Seattle, Juneau, and Honolulu. The officers in charge of these districts were known as District Commanders.

The Unification Act also required that Coast Guards-men fill in as lighthouse Keepers as needed for normal operations of the light stations. This regulation was not well received by the career lighthouse Keepers of USLHE, or by the Coast Guardsmen, who viewed such duty as a form of punishment.

When World War II was declared on December 8, 1941, all lighthouses were ordered to extinguish or reduce their beacon's light output until further notice – all lighthouses, that is, except the Tillamook Rock light. It was allowed to remain at its pre-war levels due to concerns about maritime safety on the north Oregon coast.

During the war, a Japanese submarine, I-25, shelled Fort Stevens in 1942. It was undoubtedly guided to the shore by the Tillamook Lighthouse. This bombardment was the first shelling of mainland U.S. Territory by a foreign power since the American Revolution. Fortunately, there were no casualties.

There is not much other information available about lighthouses during wartime, especially during World War II. Most of the lighthouse Keepers used their towers as lookout posts, searching the horizon for any enemy shipping. The only action report was on March 15, 1942, when the U.S. Lighthouse Service/U.S. Coast Guard tender *Acacia* was sunk by the German submarine U-161.

After the war, with maintenance and repair costs continuing to increase (the Tillamook Lighthouse was the most expensive station to operate in the entire system), and with the advent of better radar systems, and the fact that Tilly was no longer near the steamer lanes, the Coast Guard decided to close the station.

Terrible Tilly shone her light for 77 years before being replaced by a red whistle buoy, anchored one mile seaward of the Rock. It is interesting to note that, during her many years of service, from construction to operation, no woman ever set foot on the Rock. At the time, the lighthouse station was considered just too dangerous for the fairer sex.

On September 1, 1957, the last Keeper, Oswald Allik, who had served 20 years at the station, turned off the light, and penned the following final entry in the logbook:

Farewell, Tillamook Rock Light Station. An era has ended. With this final entry, and not without sentiment, I return thee to the elements. You, one of the most notorious and yet fascinating of the sea-swept sentinels in the world; long the friend of the tempest-tossed mariner. Through howling gale, thick fog and driving rain your beacon has been a star of hope and your foghorn a voice of encouragement. May the elements of nature be kind to you. For 77 years you have beamed your light across desolate acres of ocean. Keepers have come and gone; men lived and died; but you were faithful to the end. May your sunset years be good years. Your purpose is now only a symbol, but the lives you have saved and the service you have rendered are worthy of the highest respect. A protector of life and property to all, may old-timers, newcomers and travelers along the way pause from the shore in memory of your humanitarian role.

Mr. Allik, the last Keeper, enjoyed his life on the station so much that he offered to rent the lighthouse back from the Coast Guard as his personal residence. The Government turned his request down, but did hire him as the last Head Keeper of Heceta Head Lighthouse near Florence, Oregon.

Lighthouse Keeper coming to
work via Breeches Buoy in 1945

Those Keepers who served at the Tillamook Station:
(Only USLHE employees are listed here)

Head Keepers: Albert Roeder (1881), George M. Rowe (1881
– 1882), Fred B. Cosper (1882), C.D. Varnum (1882 – 1884),
Joseph Hornung (1884 – 1887), Charles H. Davis (1887), George
Hunt (1887 – 1892), Rasmus Petersen (1892 –1893), Hans P.
Score (1893), Rasmus Petersen (1893 – 1894), Marinus A.
Stream (1894), Alexander K. Pesonen (1894 – 1898), Axel
Rustad (1898 – 1900), George H. Stillwell (1900 – 1903),
William T. Langlois (1903 – 1910), William Dahlgren (1910 –
1919), Robert Gerlof (1919 – 1928), William Hill (at least 1930
– 1936), Ed Laschinger (at least 1939 – at least 1940), George H.
Wheeler (1942 – 1952), Oswald Allick (1952 – 1957).

First Assistant: J.N. Stark (1881), Thomas Jones (1881 –
1882), John P. Patterson (1882), C.D. Varnum (1882), Stephen
H. Collins (1882 – 1883), Marinus A. Stream (1883), John
Sandstrom (1883 – 1884), Joseph Hornung (1884), Nathaniel
Jones (1884 – 1885), Charles H. Davis (1885 – 1887), John M.
Flynn (1887 – 1888), Christian Zauner (1888 – 1889), Rasmus
Petersen (1889 – 1892), Hans P. Score (1892 – 1893), Alexander
K. Pesonen (1893 – 1894), Axel Rustad (1894 – 1898), George
G. Crawford (1898), George H. Stillwell (1898 – 1900), Daniel
R. Hurlbut (1900), Lars F. Amundson (1900 – 1905), William
Dahlgren (1905 – 1910), Robert Gerlof (1910 – 1919), Howard
L. Hansen (1919 – at least 1921), Charles N. Rousseau (at least
1924), George H. Wheeler (1930 – 1932), William Gadsby
(1933 – 1934), George H. Wheeler (1936 – 1942), Oswald
Allick (– 1952).

Second Assistant: Thomas Jones (1881), John P. Patterson
(1881 – 1882), Stephen H. Collins (1882), Marinus A. Stream
(1882 – 1883), John Sandstrom (1883), George W. Way (1883 –
1884), Nathaniel Jones (1884), Benjamin F. South (1884 –
1885), Ingvold F. Tronsen (1885), Henry A. Coe (1885), Lewis
M. Beemon (1886), Christian Zauner (1886 – 1888), Rasmus
Petersen (1888 – 1889), Louis C. Sauer (1889 – 1890), Hans P.
Score (1890 – 1892), Alexander K. Pesonen (1892 – 1893),

Axel Rustad (1893 – 1894), William F. Kissell (1894 – 1895),
James F. Barker (1895), William F. Kissell (1895 – 1896),
William T. Langlois (1896 – 1899), Lars F. Amundson (1899 –
1900), Gustaf A. Nikander (1900 – 1903), William Dahlgren
(1903 – 1905), Gust Jansen (1905 – 1907), Robert Gerlof (1907
– 1910), Thomas Jones (1911), Frank C. Hammond (1911 –
1916), Albert Beyer (at least 1917 - at least 1918), Walter T.
Lawrence (1919 – 1921), Criss C. Waters (1923), Teofil
Milkowski (at least 1924), George L. Burroughs (1926 – 1928),
Archie G. Cameron (1930 – 1931), Charles B. Hall (1931),
William Gadsby (1933), Henry Jenkins (1933 – 1935), Grady
Farrington (1935), Oswald Allick (at least 1939 – at least 1940).

Third Assistant: Lewis J. Mauley (1881), John P. Patterson
(1881), Stephen H. Collins (1881 – 1882), Daniel H.O. Brien
(1882 – 1883), Edmond Quinn (1883), Charles Bjorling (1883 –
1884), Charles F. Graham (1884), Benjamin F. South (1884),
James Doody (1884), Ingvold F. Tronsen (1884 – 1885), Henry
A. Coe (1885), John C. Themiley (1885), James H. Martin (1885
– 1888), Louis C. Sauer (1889), Henry C. York (1889), Hans P.
Score (1890), Henry C. Cook (1890 – 1893), George G.
Crawford (1893), William F. Kissell (1894), Joseph Burchall
(1895 – 1896), Olaf L. Hansen (1896), William T. Langlois
(1896), George G. Crawford (1896 – 1898), Lars F. Ammundson
(1898 – 1899), Gustaf A. Nikander (1899 – 1900), Thomas
Gibson (1900 – 1901), William Dahlgren (1901 – 1903), Joseph
W. Leonard (1903), Gust Jansen (1903 – 1905), Robert Gerlof
(1905 – 1907), Alex Sanders (1907 – 1908), A. Nielsen (1908 –
1910), W.H. Stark (1910 – 1911), John L. Forty (1911), Guy C.
Martin (1911 – at least 1912), Charles Miller (at least 1913),
Axel E. Andresen (at least 1915), Gardner Tibbetts (at least
1917), Orlo E. Hayward (1921), Criss C. Waters (1923), Charles
D. Whitehead (1924), George L. Burroughs (1924 – 1926),
George H. Wheeler (1929 – 1930), Archie G. Cameron (1930),
Albert H. Johnson (1930 – 1931), Floyd H. Hiller (1931) ,
Raymond Lund (1933 – 1934), Hugo Hanson (1934 –), George
H. Wheeler (1935 – 1936), Fred H. Walker (1936), Nels A.
Howe (1939), Howard W. West (1939), Roy P. Diff (at least
1940), Howard W. West (1940), Edward C. Stith (1941 - 1947).

Fourth Assistant: Rasmus Petersen (1887 – 1888), Ernest F. Booker (1888), Joseph Burchall (1894), Olaf L. Hansen (1894 – 1896), William T. Langlois (1896), George G. Crawford (1896), Edward E. Brodie (1896 – 1898), Gustaf A. Nikander (1898 – 1899), Thomas Gibson (1899 – 1900), Oscar Wiren (1900 – 1901), John Heagney (1901 – 1902), Joseph W. Leonard (1903), Gust Jansen (1903), Robert Gerlof (1903 – 1905), Charles Justen (1905– 1906), Michael F. Bergen (1906 – 1907), Alex Sanders (1907), George A. Lee (1907 – 1909), W. Monette (1909 – 1910), James E. Shaw (1912), Charles Miller (1912 –), Daniel W. Clark (at least 1913), Olaf Dahlin (at least 1913), Charles H. Bjorman (1915 – 1916), Orlo E. Hayward (1920 – 1921), Phillip E. Hedden (1923 – 1924), Charles D. Whitehead (1924), George L. Burroughs (1924), Harry Oakley (1924 – 1925), Albert Beyer (1927 – 1928), George H. Wheeler (1928 – 1929), Arthur Solverson (1929 – 1930), Albert H. Johnson (1930), Gordon Hodge (1930 – 1931), Richmond E. Umdenstock (1932), Raymond Lund (1933), Werner Storm (at least 1934), Nels A. Howe (1938 – 1939), Lon Haynes (1954 – 1956).

One of the oldest known photographs of the
Tillamook Rock Lighthouse, around 1890

Chapter Nine

Tilly Today

After Tilly was closed permanently, the Coast Guard returned to the island and removed anything of value, as instructed by the District Commander. They actually hauled away very little: the aerial beacon in the lantern room, the seldom-used New Bedford whaleboat, a set of signal flags, and filing cabinets filled with documentation from 77 years of operation. What they left behind was surprising: all of the diesel and electronic equipment, all of the hand and power tools, all of the appliances and furnishings, including the bedding, blankets, and clothing, and the entire kitchen, right down to the pots and pans. Most of the items that stayed on the island had taken years to accumulate, like the weather station and the ship-to-shore radio equipment. When the Coast Guard sailed away, the only thing the station lacked was a beacon in the tower and the Keepers to operate it.

Photo: Neal Maine ©Pacific Light Images
Tilly Today, abandoned and derelict

The Tillamook Rock Lighthouse was placed up for sale by the General Services Administration in 1959, with a listing as 'surplus property.'

Five men from Las Vegas purchased the lighthouse at a bid sale that year for $5,600. Three of the men visited the lighthouse a few weeks after the purchase, but it is believed they never again set foot on the island or funded any improvements. The Las Vegas consortium was tight lipped about why they wanted the island, which caused many of the local residents to speculate that they were planning to build a casino on the monolith. This would have been a very impractical idea as, by then, the only way on or off the island was via helicopter.

Terrible Tilly continued her timeless reputation after retirement. In 1964, a man was swept overboard while rounding the island in a small boat. His body was never recovered.

In 1973, Mr. G. Hupman, a New York-based executive with General Electric, purchased the lighthouse from the Las Vegas consortium for $11,000. His stated purpose for buying the property was to retain ties to Oregon, where his family had lived for a few years in the late 1960s. He planned to make the lighthouse his vacation home. Mr. Hupman and family cleaned up the station and spent a few nights on the island but they never returned again.

For many years, the lighthouse remained vacant, which caused the local residents to speculate again about what might happen to Tilly. Many said that McDonald's wanted the island for a 3-D billboard promoting the golden arches. Others believed the station would soon become a bed and breakfast for the super-rich. The old lighthouse and her many rumors were often the talk of the coastal towns.

In 1978, Max M. Shillock, Jr. purchased the lighthouse from Hupman for $27,000, but he was forced to cede the title to a Mr. Goolsby, whom he had reportedly swindled out of a large sum of money.

In 1980, Mr. Goolsby sold the lighthouse for $50,000 to real estate developers Mimi Morissette and Cathy Riley, backed by a group of investors. Under Morissette's direction, the structure was gutted and turned into 'Eternity at Sea Columbarium'. Interested parties could have their ashes placed inside the lighthouse, with prices varying from $1,000 for placement in the derrick room to $5,000 for a prime spot in the lantern room. With an estimated capacity of a few hundred thousand still remaining, the lighthouse seemed to be not only a self-sustaining project but a profitable business opportunity.

The property owners lost their license to operate as a columbarium in 1999, when they were late with their license renewal. In 2005, an application for a new license was rejected, due to inaccurate record keeping and improper storage of urns. Addressing concerns that urns were not well protected, Morissette, whose parents are inurned at the lighthouse, allegedly said; "People ask me what if a tsunami hits the lighthouse, and I tell every person their second choice better be to be buried at sea." Eternity at Sea still plans to raise additional money and construct niches in titanium to store some 300,000 urns. To date, only about 30 urns have been placed in the lighthouse, and vandals reportedly stole two of those in 1991. More information about Eternity at Sea Columbarium can be found in the New York Times article in Chapter 10.

Today, access to the site is severely limited, with helicopter landings the only way to access the Rock. It is off-limits even to the owners during the seabird nesting season (March 15th through September 2nd). The structure was listed on the National Register of Historic Places in 1981, and is part of the Oregon Islands National Wildlife Refuge. Being listed on the Historical rolls removes the property from all county and state taxes. Therefore, the owners of the lighthouse have not had to pay any property taxes for almost four decades.

It's a morbid reality, but this bleak Alcatraz for souls still has urns of remains inside the old station, 'Honorary Lighthouse Keepers' as Eternity at Sea called them. Today, the island is returning to its natural state as a habitat for seabirds and sea lions, and is inaccessible to everyone.

There is record of how many lives Tillamook Rock Lighthouse saved during her 77 year career. The number is most likely in the thousands, if not more. History gave her the disparaging nickname of Terrible Tilly, mainly because of the raging storms she endured. And endure them she did. The station was built nearly 140 years ago and, remarkably, she still stands. Granted, she is showing her age but, despite her decline, she will always be rich in history. So we forgive her nickname and take pride in her accomplishments; the historic and legendary *Tillamook Rock Lighthouse – tall, proud and strong.*

Chapter Ten
Tilly: News of Note

The 1894 Storm and Damage:
Astoria Daily Budget, Friday, December 14, 1894, Evening Edition

Tillamook Light: The Latest Report Brought by the *Columbine*, (lighthouse tender). The Storm Sunday Did Considerable Damage! The Kitchen Was Wrecked and Water Deep on the Floor of the Living Rooms

A report that there has been a fierce storm at Tillamook Rock and the light has not been burning, was confirmed by the report from the officers of the *Columbine* who went there yesterday to inspect matters and returned last evening.

The *Columbine* arrived at the rock about 2 o'clock yesterday morning but on account of the turbulence of the water would not attempt to land. Keeper Passonen and his three assistants were still on the rock and hailed the good ship with joy.

Once or twice they were within talking distance of the men on the rock and managed to arrange with the keeper for a transfer of his report to the vessel. This was done by placing the report in a tightly corked bottle, secured to a float which was thrown far out into the sea. It floated alongside and was picked up. A member of the crew, unrolled several sheets of official paper and allowed the reporter to read it. It is a thrilling account of Sunday's dangerous storm when for hours the brave watchmen on lonely Tillamook Rock, listened to the awful howling of the wind and waters, trembling each moment for fear that the high tower would tumble over into the sea and carry everything with it. Waves rose all around them like great mountains.

Although the top of the rock is fully 88 feet above extreme high tide, monster seas broke over it. At one time when the hurricane was at its worst, amidst a most awful roaring of the angry waters, a great wall of water struck the side of the rock with such force that it trembled as if from a violent shock of earthquake. As the mountain of water struck the rock, it shot upwards, how high the keepers inside the lighthouse were unable to say, but all was dark for a moment with an awful crash of breaking glass sounded above followed instantly by a terrible noise as if the whole ocean had gone skyward and come down directly on the roof of the lighthouse.

By this time it seemed to the keepers that their time had come and they were for a moment unable to make out whether they were still on the rock or floating off on the crest of the receding wave. The water in their living room was now four feet deep and the furniture was floating about the place. As soon as they are partially recovered from the onslaught, they made a hasty examination which revealed their sad state of affairs. In the fog horn room a mark on the wall showed that water had entered to a depth of six feet and the engine for the fog horn was soaked, damaged and would not work.

For the fresh water, the pump on the cistern was out of service and there was sea water now mixed with the fresh drinking water. We were in trouble! In the kitchen, a remarkable state of affairs confronted us. Everything in the room was soaked. Every time a huge wave over-washed the building, more water poured through a big hole in the roof. The hole had been made by a great boulder hundreds of pounds in weight that came crashing through. The kitchen stove was a total wreck and nearly all the pots and pans were missing, having been washed right out the broken windows as the water receded. Everything in the way of edibles except stock of canned goods was ruined. There had been two new loaves of bread on the table and these had disappeared. Over the hallway the roof was also shattered and we could see the sky.

The most startling sight was when the men ascended into the tower at the top of which was the great Fresnel First Order lens and lamp. This was 136 feet above the ocean. The windows were all broken and panes in the lens were broken. The clock machinery was beyond immediate repair. It had almost collapsed with the force of the water that hit it. In the tower we found some of the rocks that had been hurled by the sea into the lantern. One of these was about the size of a watermelon and weighed about 30 pounds. Ordinary lanterns were hung out as emergency lights every night but these had none of the power of the giant lens. In fact, the lanterns seemed only as faint glimmers in the night. The men on the rock were able to report they were all well and had enough canned food to last a few days but it would have to be eaten cold. The *Columbine* was expected to return to Tillamook Rock in a few days and if there was a chance of making a landing, some of the crew would do so, but the landing hook, and derrick on the rock, was broken. A newspaper account said the men on the rock acted with great coolness and bravery.

𝕿𝖍𝖊 𝕺𝖗𝖊𝖌𝖔𝖓𝖎𝖆𝖓 Jan. 17, 1911

Seas Strike Lighthouse: Damage Done on Top of Tillamook Rock Reported

Astoria, Ore. - One panel was gone from the iron railing around the rock and a window was broken in the lower hallway of the lighthouse was the damage wrought by a monstrous wave that swept Tillamook Rock during the last severe storm off the Oregon coast, but none of the men on the rock sustained injuries and there was no harm to other parts of the station, according to Commander Endicott, Inspector of the Seventeenth Lighthouse District. He succeeded in gaining the rock Sunday after waiting for favorable weather since early last fall. The trip was made aboard the tender *Manzanita*.

Warning: *Readers should not try this swim! It would be foolish, dangerous and illegal!*

July 26, 1934

Headline: **Graphic Story of Swim as Told By Eyewitness**
Sub Headline: **Lifeguards Finish Swim To Tillamook Rock After Long Struggle In Frigid Waters Of The Pacific Ocean**

"They are crazy to try it! Nine miles in that cold Pacific-over the roughest stretch of water you can find?? Not me. I wouldn't even go along in the boat."

That was what they were saying Friday when it was learned that Wally Hug and Jim Reed, lifeguards, had started the long swim to Tillamook Rock. We couldn't all go but here is the "play-by-play" story of the swim.4:30 a.m. Friday, July 20, the Little Gem café. Wally Hug, Jim Reed and Bill Hoops are already gathered at the counter for breakfast. We enter. What will we have? Coffee? There's something about the bounding deep which doesn't make a full stomach seem so good. 5:30 a.m., in the heating plant of Oates' Baths. The boys are stripped and applying axel grease – yes, just plain axle grease to help them withstand the cold.

The boat, a small skiff is waiting for us beyond The Tides, so with Bill Hoops we ride out, launch the boat and find the launching smoother than might have been expected. We pull along up the coast until nearly opposite the Turnaround. A tanned muscular arm flashes on the flank of a large green wave.

"There they are!" Bill shouts.

Bill at the oars, sweating profusely: "How's it going fellows?"

Jim Reed replies: "Fine, jump in and cool off."

6:45 a.m. The swimmers swing close aboard and ask if the beef broth is warm. A short pause while they rinse out their mouths and again the steady stroking.

Sea Lion Ahoy

7:00 a.m. "Any sea lions?" Wally wants to know through chattering teeth. Yes, at the end of the hour the cold is intense.

"No sea lions." Bill replies. But in a lower tone to us, "Look out there, no farther north – see that?"

A tan and gray sea lion flashes for a moment on the flank of a wave and disappears.

"How you feeling?"

Jim Reed's white teeth flash in a smile and he nods. No time for wasted breath. Wally Hug gags, and answers "sick."

"What's the matter, sea-sick?"

"Yeah."

A long pause while Wally Hug overcomes the nausea which has swept on him as a result of the salt water and waving sea, because the sea-green rollers are going eight or ten feet high.

Wally is swimming stronger now that he feels better. Another pause for broth and they're off, working hard, determined not to quit. Slowly – so slowly the time seems an eternity, the grim forbidding walls of the Death Trap slip away to the northward.

"How close are we?"

This at 8 a.m. "An hour and a half or two hours."

Discouraging news to us, but the boys only increase their pace a little. A sprint to warm up, then they roll over on their backs to rest while we idle at the oars, barely keeping headway to hold the bow into the swells.

Another half hour slips past during which their arms fall heavier, heavier into the water. Like lead, it seems, the stroke slow, but infinitely sure. Their faces are turning white now and against the pallid background their lips are black with cold.

Another pause for broth, but they are so stiff they cannot hold the cups.

More minutes as long as hours. The lighthouse is a bulking reality now. A half hour at the most. Suddenly our boat begins to rock and jump, nice manipulation of the oars is necessary to keep the waves from slopping over the side and swamping us. A rip tide, Bill explains. Then calls out to the swimmers. They're O.K., and the current feels warmer. A pitiful difference of one or two degrees, but they're game.

Rip Tide Crossed

The strain of making the rip tide which was only a hundred feet across has told on them. We gained about 300 yards to the south while making a hundred toward our destination.

The south current is carrying us toward the light rapidly and it seems to grow and take form as a photographic print does in solution. The sun is shining hot.

They're being carried by! No chance a hundred yards from the light, fighting 15 minutes and not a foot nearer.

Take 'em aboard Bill, we can make it over if were careful.

A hail from the rock where steam has been up in the winch since 6 o'clock. Swing in under the basket. The white boom turns majestically above our heads while the ocean churns info froth below u and occasional waves slop over the side. The basket's down! Wally tumbles into it. Jim reaches out for the rope. The boat rocks drunkenly, Bill works ceaselessly at the oars, the basket swings toward the rock and Jim's grip weakens. For a terrifying moment he balances between sky and sea on the rim of the basket. Will he make it? His greased fingers, a lurch of the basket and he tumbles into it. "Haul away!"

We're next. We make a line fast to the boat and step into the basket. Up she goes! The boat fades to a speck and we soar above the creaming waves like gulls. Firm ground.

Hot baths, hot meal and the swimmers are ready to start back to work on the beach all afternoon protecting lives. They even insist upon taking their trick at the oars!

Sheer nerve, supreme physical ability and a new record has been hung up.

Wallace Hug and Jim Reed are the first men to ever swim from the Turnaround at Seaside to the Tillamook Rock and in letters of ink, but letters of gold to the beholder, these facts are entered forever in the visitor's book at the Tillamook Light and the log for the day. July 20, 1934. *Story by Fulton Travis, Seaside Signal*

The New York Times

By WILLIAM YARDLEY OCT. 24, 2007

Headline: **Terrible Tillie, Where the Departed Rest Not Quite in Peace**

CANNON BEACH, Ore. — Tillamook Rock Lighthouse, a mile off the Oregon coast and dark for half a century, would be just another postcard from the past if not for all the dead people inside.

Peace at the last on an island in the Pacific is what they said they wanted; and, if they paid anywhere from $1,000 to $2,500 to have their cremated ashes placed in the lighthouse, that is what they were promised.

"That's what she talked about for years," Terri Reynolds recalled of her mother, Thelma, who was 87 when she died in 2004, many years after having paid to place her ashes in the lighthouse. "'All you'll have to do is go to Cannon Beach and look out there and you'll know where I'm at,' she said."

Aerial View: Eternity by the Sea Columbarium

The big rock on which the lighthouse was built in the 1880s has never made for much of a sanctuary. About 20 miles south of the mouth of the Columbia River, it becomes an angry acre of basalt when big ocean waves slam across it. The lighthouse soon became known as Terrible Tillie. Dangerous and expensive to operate, it was decommissioned in 1957.

The rock has long since been reclaimed by cormorants and common murres, and the lighthouse is now the privately owned Eternity by the Sea Columbarium. Except that neither eternity nor the sea is cooperating.

After a quarter century of soliciting souls, and after placing about 30 urns in the lighthouse, Eternity by the Sea has lost its license. The rock and the lighthouse are caked in guano, and the roof is leaking.

A state board says the owners have not kept accurate records of people placed there and that because urns sit on boards and concrete blocks, not in niches, the lighthouse does not even qualify as a columbarium.

Two urns were lost years ago when vandals reportedly broke open the doors. Birds quickly flew in and built nests before the doors were repaired.

Some families with relatives who were inurned there are upset. So are others whose parents made payments before they died, only to have their children learn that the columbarium could not legally accept any more "honorary lighthouse keepers." The owners say that they have done nothing wrong, and that the state unfairly shut them down.

Even if the place were patched up tomorrow and allowed back into business, no one would be allowed to visit. A helicopter is the only means of transport; and, because Tillamook Rock is a privately owned part of the Oregon Coast National Wildlife Refuge Complex, it is even off limits to its owners during the mild weather of spring and summer when seabirds are nesting.

Nevertheless, the Web site for Eternity by the Sea still makes its pitch. "Honorary Lighthouse Keepers Wanted," it says. "We are currently not accepting new keepers but you can add your name to a waiting list where you will be notified when we can offer 'Columbarium Niche Options.' All future keepers will be offered a discount if their name is on this waiting list."

Ms. Reynolds and her sister, Jan Keffer, say they were misled by the lighthouse owners and have drafted a complaint to the Oregon Department of Justice.

Because the lighthouse lost its license in 1999 and was rejected in 2005 after it applied for a new one, Thelma Reynolds's ashes are kept by Ms. Keffer in Arizona. The daughters say the principal owner of the lighthouse, Mimi Morissette, a real estate developer near Hood River, Ore., has said she would return the $1,000 their mother paid in 1980, but with no interest. Money, they say, is not the issue.

"What's important is to follow the wishes of the loved ones," Terri Reynolds said.

Ms. Morissette bought the lighthouse in 1980 with a group of investors for $50,000 and began promoting it as a columbarium.

Over the years, she said, she has presold about 100 urns, though perhaps fewer, and she said most of the money had gone to maintenance and legal fees.

She said she has returned three deposits, though she would not say to whom, and the identity of people whose ashes are stored at the lighthouse is not public record. In 2005, according to the state, the balance in the columbarium's endowment was $451.51.

Ms. Morissette said the state was the problem, not her, and that the lighthouse was essentially shut down for a technical violation, having been late in renewing its license back in the 1990s. She said the Oregon Mortuary and Cemetery Board, which controls the licensing process, was deliberately keeping the lighthouse out of the increasingly lucrative industry of storing ashes, what those in the business call cremains.

Location View: Eternity by the Sea Columbarium

Cremation has become much more common across the country and particularly in the Northwest. In Oregon, said David J. Koach, executive director of the Mortuary and Cemetery Board, about 65 percent of people now choose cremation, about twice the national rate.

In 1975, the state rate was about 15 percent. But Mr. Koach rejected the assertion that the board, whose members are appointed by the governor, was somehow protecting others in the industry when it rejected the application for a new license.

He cited a 23-page summary of the decision, which noted that investigators for the board found multiple violations that included poor record-keeping and improper storage of urns.

"There's no there there," Mr. Koach said. "There aren't any niches. How can they sell them if they're not there?"

Ms. Morissette said she was planning a major renovation next spring, before the migratory birds return. Her long-range plans for the lighthouse remain ambitious: raising about $1 million, reapplying for a license or skipping that process altogether, and constructing walls of niches in titanium that could store 300,000 urns.

As for concerns that the current urns are not well protected, she said, "People ask me what if a tsunami hits the lighthouse, and I tell every person their second choice better be to be buried at sea."

Waves and the birds will certainly continue to come. Jerry Jeffs, whose mother, Nora Bailey Knight, bought an urn back in the 1980s and was placed in the lighthouse after she died in 1991, said she worried about how her stylish mother, a former buyer for a department store, was withstanding the elements.

"She didn't even like bird poop on her car," Ms. Jeffs said.

Chapter Eleven
TALES OF TILLY: KEEPER'S OPEN LETTER
by Howard L. Hansen

Publicity about the decommissioning of the Tillamook Rock Lighthouse in 1957 was widespread, reaching even to foreign publications. The old sentinel had long been a vital part of Oregon's history, even though it was separated from the mainland by a mile of turbulent seas. Oregonians loved the old lighthouse, with all its majesty and mystery. Many memories were rekindled and stories published concerning the Rock. Mrs. W.W. Banks, while searching through some old papers, discovered a long-forgotten letter among her possessions. Its contents were published in the Seaside Signal, in 1968, telling of early life on the monolith. The letter was written from Tillamook Rock Light on November 27, 1919, by the first assistant lighthouse Keeper, concerning Mrs. Banks's letter written many years early, when she lived in Ecola, Oregon. Here, in his own words, is what the keeper had to say about living and surviving on the Rock:

Received your letter asking for information about our light, so will try and describe it. We are out here on a lone rock about one mile from shore. We have no communication with shore only when one of the tenders brings us provisions and mail-sometimes once a month and sometimes in the winter time we are here 60 to 70 days without a boat.

The light is about 130 feet above the water. Seas come over this in the winter time with such force as to break the heavy plate glass around the lens, putting out the light and causing considerable work to get wooden shutters in the place where the glass is broken out.

The lens has twenty-four bulls-eyes that throw out the rays of light, revolving around once every two minutes, causing a flash every five seconds. The light is a vapor light on the same principle as these mantle lamps they pump up with air and heat a little tube so as to generate a kind of gas. After going through the lens this light has developed 48,000 candle power. The light is lighted at sundown and runs until sunrise.

The buildings are built of stone and brick. The main building is made of stone blocks a foot square and three feet long, each block being fastened to the others with copper bars so as to stand the pounding of the sea. The tower rises from the center of the building. There are eight rooms beside the tower. These are our quarters, kitchen, storeroom and office.

The siren room is built onto the west end of the main building. There are two eighteen-horse-power semi-diesel engines that run the compressors which pump air into a big tank. This tank, when running the fog siren, is kept at 40 pounds pressure. A valve is opened at regular times by the engine to let the compressed air rush into the siren. The siren is composed of two brass cylinders, one revolving inside of the other, caused by the air rushing through them. This siren is run whenever it is so foggy that we cannot see five miles.

In landing on the rock we have a derrick that we swing out with a steam donkey and lower a cage down to the lifeboat from the tenders. Our provisions or men get into this cage and are hoisted up. Sometimes when the cage is lowered down they miss the boat, with the result that whoever happens to be in it gets wet.

There are five men allowed to this station, four men on the rock with one man on shore on his vacation. At this time there are five of us on the rock. The keeper is a man 61 years of age, the other four are from 18 to 23. One of the young men spent 10 months in France with the army, so we have some very interesting stories after work.

We spend the forenoons cleaning up around the station, keeping everything in the very best of shape, and to help pass the time away. The afternoons we have to ourselves to read or pass the time as we please. In the wintertime it gets rather lonesome as we have to keep the windows all closed tight and cannot get outside of the house very often. You have very likely heard stories of men going crazy out here and also that there is a big iron band around the rock to hold it together. These stories are all made up by somebody who had so much spare time that he did not know what else to do.

We all are glad to know that there is somebody who can watch our light and listen to our fog siren and who takes enough interest in-us to write asking for information. Although we may not be able to get over to the beach to see our nearest neighbors, by next summer we will have a telephone cable between here and there. Some 25 years ago there was a telegraph cable from here to shore but it did not last long. It broke and was never replaced.

You asked why it was a revolving light instead of stationary. The main reason is that a stationary light is very often mistaken for some other light and sometimes is the cause of a wreck.

Mr. Howard L. Hansen
First assistant Lighthouse keeper
November 27, 1919

Chapter Twelve
TALES OF TILLY: RESCUE FROM THE ROCK
by Brian D. Ratty

With trees snapping and winds howling in the many disastrous coastal storms, my mind raced back to my grandfather, Harry, and his daring rescue off the Tillamook Rock Lighthouse in 1934.

As a young boy in the early 1950's, I remember visiting my grandparent's home in west Portland where, over the fireplace mantel, hung two black and white photographs that Harry had neatly framed. These images, which had appeared in the *National Geographic Magazine* in August of 1936, helped him tell his story of being rescued from the Rock. After his death in 1970, those photos and his story became just a foggy memory to me. Then, last year, a cousin loaned me a tattered box full of family memorabilia. Deep inside, I found both the yellowing photographs and my grandfather's story on faded newspaper clip-pings. With the aid of today's technology, I was able to restore both the images and the story of his daring rescue.

In the 1930's, Harry Ratty worked for the Lighthouse Service as a maintenance engineer. He traveled from Cape Disappointment to Coos Bay, repairing the many lighthouses that dotted the region. These bright white sentinels were manned 24-7 by Keepers who spent months on the station. Harry and his crews kept their lights burning, the fog horns blasting, and the Keepers safe from the terrible elements.

My grandfather was a quiet man with that Oregon spirit of rugged independence. Just after the turn of the century, he entered the building trades and helped shape the Portland skyline with structures like the J.K. Gill Building, the Lipman Wolfe Building and the old Multnomah Hotel. In 1928, he helped build the Big Dipper roller coaster at Jantzen Beach Amusement Park.

Coincidentally, my father Dudley (also a contractor) tore down that same coaster in 1972. Harry also worked on the Bonneville Dam and, during World War II, was in charge of the civilian contractors at the Warrenton Naval Air Station on the north coast. But, of all of his accomplishments, it was the Rock that he talked about the most.

In October of 1934, a violent storm swept over the Rock, causing over $5,000 damage to the lighthouse. As the storm finally retreated, Harry and his crew were landed on the Rock via lighthouse tender. A few weeks later, while extensive repairs were being made, a second ferocious storm blew up from the south. This one had winds of over 75 mph and sent 60 pound boulders smashing against the light tower and stone building. Power was lost again, as was the telephone cable to shore. With windows broken, rain and sea pouring in, and the light's Fresnel lens shattered, the four marooned Keepers and five-man work party rode out the gale for almost five days. Finally, one of the Keepers, a ham radio operator, made contact with shore for rescue. During this time, Harry, a crew member and one of the other Keepers were taken seriously ill as a result of exposure. A rescue boat was sent but, after two days of unsuccessful attempts to remove them from the Rock, the lighthouse tender *Rose* was dispatched. In dangerous, stormy waters, she was able to shoot a rope line to the lighthouse and rig up a breeches buoy from the Rock to her deck. Riding the breeches buoy from the lighthouse, over the churning waters, to the pitching deck of the *Rose* was an experience my grand-father would never forget. By the time Harry (pictured) reached the tender, riding just over the bobbing safety boat, his shoes were wet and his nerves frayed. Aboard the tender was a Coast Guard photographer, who took the pictures. Harry and four others were removed from the lighthouse in this manner while replacement crews and supplies were sent back up. My grandfather and two of the others were sent on to Astoria for medical treatment.

Harry Ratty in breeches buoy 1934

This story of rescue was national news and made the front pages of many newspapers. The box of clippings and family memorabilia brings new meaning to Grandfather Harry's recollections and the importance of struggling through any 'storm.'

Harry Ratty – right front - Next to Head Lighthouse
Keeper William Hill. Note sandbags on the left.

Digging deeper into this box, I also found a tattered copy of a Western Union telegram addressed to Harry while he was recovering at the Astoria hospital. It was a message from his wife, Elsie, (my grandmother), still back in Portland. It simply read:

Glad you are well –stop- Come home soon -stop- Bills need to be paid –stop.

So much for Harry's 15 seconds of fame and his rescue from the Rock!

In 1957 the lighthouse was decommissioned and the island sold.

Chapter Thirteen
TALES OF TILLY: EXILED
by James A. Gibbs

The lighthouse keeper has gone the way of the iceman and the blacksmith, but his story remains. Here are the unique adventures I experienced as a lighthouse keeper on a sea-girt piece of real estate off Oregon's timeless shores. Since that adventure at Tillamook Rock lighthouse, more than a couple of decades have passed, during which automation, computerization and many other remarkable innovations, such as television, have become an accepted way of life.

Since my experiences, the main characters have all passed on and the infamous "Terrible Tilly" was long ago bugled out of active service. Reduced from riches to rags since its retirement in 1957, the decaying structure has gone through three private owners, each of which fought a futile battle to preserve what has become a white elephant. The rock defies all efforts at revival, due in great part to its geographical inaccessibility.

Through binding decree, the Coast Guard in 1957 declared that the rusting lantern room should never again display a light in its crown. As the elements go about their inevitable work of destruction, legions of seabirds zero in on the timeless crag, claiming it as their rookery and 'general-purpose air terminal, whitening the precipitous rock with their droppings.

But let us go back to the hectic days of 1945 when World War II was winding down. I remember one winter morning well cold, sullen, the wind blasts cutting like a whetted knife. The engine purred as the 52-foot motor lifeboat pitched and rolled her way toward the Columbia River bar. Gripping the railing, I looked at the ominous clouds hanging precariously like the top of a huge circus tent, painting the heaving sea an eerie gray. Toward the horizon it was as if a deep, black ditch dropped off into nothingness. The wind gusts nipped off the crests of the mountainous swells, blowing the spume into a lather of spray. Astern, beyond our erratic wake, shoal waters stretched endlessly away to the north and south. Lost in the murky distance were the Coast Guard station behind Point Adams and the skylines of Astoria and Ilwaco. As the seas increased in intensity, the shuddering craft responded to the thrust of the screw, nosing over a titanic roller abreast the jetty, dropping in a trough, and then climbing to the peak of another roller.

In my stomach, a total of two fried eggs rested uneasily. The grizzled helmsman glanced at me period-ically, seeming to enjoy the green glow at my gills. He laughed as he told me the worst was yet to come. A distorted smile came over my face, and a burning sensation gripped my interior.

My jovial shipmate was joined shortly by the bosun, who emerged from the hatch gnawing on a piece of greasy meat. After a few casual remarks he turned toward me.

"Tillamook Rock," he muttered, "I wouldn't take that duty on a bet."

My attention was diverted. I was more concerned at the moment about keeping the eggs down than pondering his trite remark.

"You can have the rock," he persisted, "I don't want any part of it."

"That makes two of us," remarked his cohort.

I tried to pretend I wasn't much interested, but my ears automatically stood at attention for I knew virtually nothing of the place except that vacancies were reserved for Cost-guard troublemakers.

"Remember the time we took the guy off the rock in a strait jacket?" said the bosun to the other.

"Yah! He was a real section eight."

By then, the lifeboat was taking it green over the bow and I renewed my hold on the nearest stanchion. Our sou'westers were matted with salt, our rubber boots sloshing in six inches of bilge water. The boat shook herself like a wet poodle as she rounded the buoy off the jetty and pursued a southerly course. Jostled about by the rushing pyramids of water, she flung herself at the opposition like a football guard. After a few hours of rigorous voyaging in that seagoing elevator, the bosun yelled in my ear.

"See that speck? That's where you're going, mate."

He handed me the glasses. I peered at the watery crests of hissing, yeasty foam. My stomach felt empty at what I saw, but probably more so because those two eggs were no longer there.

Suddenly the haze parted as if Mother Nature had waved it away. The speck grew ever larger and more ominous as the lifeboat neared. Savage breakers lashed its sides-blockbusters that had traveled miles across the Pacific only to snub their noses and explode in an awesome display of lacey spray. The chilling wind stung my inquisitive eyes as I glanced at the sea, at the sky and then back at the rock. The ocean was enormous. Obvious consternation wrinkled the faces of the lifeboat crew, though all four had probably made the run to the rock many times before.

"Better wake up!" the helmsman yelled to another of the crew sacked out below. "May be rough sledding."

The sleeping individual, doubling as cook and machinist's mate in the absence of the former, was catching some winks. His immunity to the pitch and roll was nothing short of amazing.

As the craft jockeyed closer, the dank odor of seaweed and bird droppings filled my nostrils. The bastion-like walls that rose before us were almost frightening. Seemingly casting an evil shadow over us, the ocean lifted the boat to a pinnacle and then dropped it into a bottomless pit. Barnacles and mussels, huge ones, were exposed, thick and slimy around the girth of the rock like the fouled boot topping of a monstrous merchant ship.

We had traveled some 20 miles south from the mouth of the Columbia River, and here out in the ocean, com-pletely exposed to the elements more than a mile offshore, was Tillamook Rock, one of the most unusual basaltic masses I had ever beheld. The rock at best covered less than a quarter acre at its plateau and it was filled almost entirely by the lighthouse. No place was there any vegetation. I felt I was indeed "between a rock and a hard place." The giant stone building stood nearly 100 feet above sea level, its tower I was informed, reaching 134 feet into the lowering sky, surrounded by that ever-penetrating odor one might associate with a marine graveyard.

I couldn't really believe that I was going to be a resident of such an isolated place; it seemed more like a pint-sized Alcatraz and that I was about to serve my sentence as an undesirable service man. And, admittedly, that was the reason for my new assignment. I had already been informed that those who manned this stationary ship were old-time career civil-service employees, the last of the U.S. Lighthouse Service personnel, permitted to remain in their former status when the Coast Guard took over that branch of the Commerce Department in 1939. Those doughty individuals, as I was later to find out, were better suited to such isolated duty for long periods than were the younger Coast Guardsmen like myself.

The sight before me was unlike any I had ever seen. I wondered how anyone could get onto the rock with the rise and fall of the sea being not less than ten feet. The wind was nearly 30 knots and the water rough and surging, hardly the most desirable situation for a landing. I had all I could do just to hang tight to what seemed a runaway bronc from a rodeo.

The boat crew appeared to know what they were doing, but it seemed to me that one wrong move could mean a one-way ticket to Davy Jones's Locker. Our lifeboat was like a match stick below that monolith of wave-lashed basalt, an encumbrance that had probably been shouldering a losing battle against the ocean since Noah rode the ark.

Atop the sheer walls stood three individuals peering down at us like vultures, totally absorbed in the gyrating movements of our craft which was turning in slow circles. In a small building perched on the eastern slope of the rock another man, faintly visible, worked the hoist controls. Suddenly, over the sounds of the wind and surging surf there was a grinding noise and a huge wooden boom began swinging slowly like the neck of a cautious giraffe. It halted its arc above our restless craft. A swaying cable began threading downward toward the water as our craft pitched and rolled violently, holding cautiously to the 50-foot distance from the sinister base of the bastion. When in the right position, the boat's engine began idling but the ocean's motion would not cooperate. Directed toward the fo'c'sle, it was all I could do to make my way forward.

"Here!" shouted the bosun, tapping me on the shoulder, "this is for you!"

He handed me a life ring with a pair of oversized canvas pants protruding from a hole in the center.

"Take it" he insisted, "it's a breeches buoy."

"What in blazes do I do with it?" I retorted.

"You want to get up on the rock, don't you?" he nodded my head feebly.

"Then jump into the pants and hop up on the fo'c'sle head and wait till we get under the cable hook."

Like a drunken sailor, I struggled to position, trying to keep my equilibrium with one hand and hold up my newly acquired "bloomers" with the other. With rubbery legs I finally stood erect. From my position, the top of the lighthouse seemed to touch the low-hanging clouds, but what occupied my mind was how I could hold the breeches buoy with one hand and at the same time hook the ring on the attached ropes into the cable hook. The boat moved slowly once again until we were directly under the swinging cable.

"Hook it! Hook it!" hollered the bosun.

As I reached skyward, he turned his attention to the man at the wheel.

"Look sharp! Look sharp there, or she'll be into that whirlpool. Ease off!"

The boat heeled ungraciously and rose again on a huge swell, gathering speed while every bolt seemingly wrenched in its socket.

I stood on tiptoe and grabbed for the hook. Just then the craft took a decided lurch and I went sprawling, grabbing the nearest solid thing to keep from going overboard. I could hear oaths of profanity as the boat shuddered, water pouring over the fantail. For a moment we steadied on a ridge of liquid. Too busy maneuvering the bucking craft to be concerned about me, the crew displayed their seamanship abilities in getting us back into position.

Securing the breeches buoy around my waist once again, I spread my feet apart, braced myself and waited. Again the boat came up under the cable hook.

"Grab the damn thing! Grab it!" a voice shouted at me.

This time I connected with the eyebolt, but before catching my breath, my feet went out from under me and I was dragged unceremoniously over the fo'c'sle head, ensconced in the breeches buoy. As the bosun signaled to the figure in the derrick house, I felt the ropes of the conveyance tighten. Over the side I went, floundering in the coldest water this side of solid ice. I thought my death warrant had been signed, when with a terrific jerk I ascended from the depths like a hooked fish-up, up, dangling some 75 feet above the swirling waters boiling against the defiant precipice below. For a moment I thought I had sprouted wings, but quickly realized that once yanked from the brine, my survival was now dependent on the flimsy contraption that held me between sea and sky.

Keeper Reporting For Work

The lifeboat dwindled in size below me. Strong gusts hampered the turning of the boom for what seemed an eternity as I sat there rocking, the chill wind making ice sheets of my wet clothing. When the machine in the derrick house finally mustered enough power to swing the boom, I breathed a bit easier but kept wondering why amusement park promoters had never given this invention a whirl.

When the boom finally terminated its arc, I was directly over a slab of concrete set in the black, basaltic mass. As the cable played out, the scene below flashed dismally. At the plateau of the rock the huge, square stone building, crowned by a tower, loomed ever larger. The east slope of the rock, where I was to land, slid into the ocean like the laced portion of an old man's shoe. The southern exposure was broken by a deep fissure where the breakers roared in and shot geysers of spray skyward. Dropping vertically into the sea were the precipitous north and western slopes, the latter with a definite overhang. A feeling of futility came over me, the like of which I had never before experienced. At the moment I would have given a king's ransom for a return ticket to the mainland.

As the platform came up to meet me, a pair of weathered hands reached upward and guided me to solid ground. I was joined by yet another who stood dressed in civilian clothes, a small suitcase at his side. As I struggled out of the breeches buoy, the slightly graying man with the suitcase scrambled into the conveyance. It was obvious he was eager and anxious for his shore leave. Before any words were exchanged, I watched the breeches buoy become airborne once again, then stood alone with the one who had guided me down.

"George is the name," he volunteered, "George Wheeler. Yah better get topside and get them wet duds off. Ask for Allik, he'll show you where to go."

I noted the suitcase still stood on the platform, plus a big canvas sack full of letters and packages waiting to be off-loaded. My sea bag was still aboard the lifeboat but, instead of waiting, I heeded the advice of the keeper on the landing platform and went topside, shivering as if icicles were down my back.

I left George behind, a relatively tall, large-boned individual, slightly lanky and on the 60 side of life and started up the cement stairway that had been poured into the rock. On my way, I passed the derrick house and got a better look at the man at the controls. Slight and wiry with whitish hair, he gave me a half wave while concentrating on the levers. I wanted to ask him why he dragged me through the brine, but the time wasn't right. I looked down into the watery chasm in time to see the vacationing keeper being dropped to the boat. For a time he wavered in the air and I wondered if he too would get a dunking. Fortune was with him, however, two crewmen aiding him while the man at the wheel managed to hold the boat steady.

Just as I reached the entrance to the lighthouse, I turned back once again to see a cargo net being attached to the cable hook, with supplies, mail and my sea bag contained therein.

I was impressed with the exterior of the lighthouse, solid stone blocks better than two feet thick, fit together with precision. Above the curved archway of the entrance, cut deep into the stone, were the following words:

TILLAMOOK ROCK L.H.
ERECTED 1880
LON. 124° 01' W. LAT. 45° 56'N.

It appeared that the white, painted edifice had stood well the test of time, though it was obvious everywhere I looked that Mother Nature's anger had left numerous jagged scars.

Still dripping as if out of a shower, a trail of water marked my footsteps on entering the building. A short entrance through a storm door left me standing in a spacious hallway or foyer. At the center was an iron circular staircase that wound ever upward into the tower, while bordering the hall was a series of bedrooms. I continued through the building, the thickness of the walls shutting out the sounds of the wind and sea. It felt strange to stand there alone, not hearing any human stirrings. Shortly after passing a storeroom I heard the clatter of pans and silverware and then found myself in the kitchen face to face with a third keeper, whom I assumed to be Allik. I introduced myself and told him about my dunking.

"Happens often, especially when it's rough," he said with a slight accent.

Allik was a shy, soft-spoken individual, but friendly. Estonian by birth, he said he had come over from the old Country while a young man, immediately applying for and later being accepted into government service. His first assignment duty had been aboard the Columbia River Lightship. He informed me that George was the head keeper, or as they said in Lighthouse Service language, the principal keeper. Allik, whose first name was Oswald (Ozzie), showed me to my room at the east end of the building, but did not come in.

"One rule we keep here," he said, "is we stay out of each other's bedroom. Gets pretty lonesome with no place to go and we got to respect each other's privacy."

With that, he left me at the door. I went inside the 10x10-foot room, which contained a bed and an old dresser with a linoleum of sorts on the floor. An ocean view was afforded through a single ship's porthole offering a southerly exposure. It was apparent that a window had once been where the porthole was fitted, for I was soon to learn that the fury of the southerly gales had taken its toll, repeatedly having shattered storm panes and window frames. The rugged porthole, set deep in the stone, contained inch-thick glass. Even then, I could see numerous nicks where debris had been flung against it.

As I looked around my cell, many thoughts passed through my mind and most were negative. The trance was broken with a knock at my door, but on opening it, nobody was there. Instead, my sea bag was standing at attention. I was quick to get off my wet clothes.

Everywhere I looked, the place took on more of the aspects of an insane asylum instead of what I had pictured a lighthouse to be. I wondered if they would give me a Section Eight-psychologically unfit-before completing the first hitch of my sentence. It was all I could do to keep from running back to the landing platform and pleading to be removed. In fact, I did go to the entrance again, looking out in agony as the motor lifeboat cork screwed away from the rock, plowing into heavy seas. For the first time it struck me solidly that I would be here for three long months before "the coveted time off. For one who was used to people and places, this would be a challenge. It was as if I had been exiled forever from civilization.

When night came on dark and eerie, I could see the hint of lights at the distant resorts of Seaside and Cannon Beach. I knew for the first time what men imprisoned at Alcatraz, in the center of San Francisco Bay, must have felt. Here alone was I with three career lighthouse keepers all considerably older than myself, none of whom appeared too happy to have a young Coast Guardsman added to their ranks-a replacement for another who had failed to endure the loneliness and privation.

After I had collected my thoughts, and before being schooled in my assignments, my tour of the lighthouse continued. The structure was 64x45 feet, slightly indented at the western extremity, which consisted of a 16x22-foot fog signal room where the generators and compressors for the fog sirens were located. A coal bin and oil-storage tanks were also there, plus a half-filled punching bag hanging from the ceiling. A concrete walk about 12 feet wide rimmed the entire structure, with little room left for anything else at the plateau of the rock. Huge metal fuel and water tanks were located outside the structure at the eastern and western ends, and I couldn't help noticing the rust streaks from the salt air that had attacked everything made of metal, including the railing.

The rear door was at the northwesterly section of the building, below which was a straight 90-foot drop to the ocean. The northeast portion contained a small paint and storage locker and tiny but solid, reinforced, masonry privy. Talk about your brick outhouses-this one capped them all. Curiosity led me to inspect and what I saw inside made me shudder. It was a one-holer, the hole dropping directly to the ocean, and the wind vacuum coming up through it was like a small tornado. I got to thinking that sitting on that wind tunnel could greatly hamper nature's calling. I worried about that until I went back into the fog signal room and discovered that there was a bathroom, be it ever so small, with a toilet and a vintage bathtub. Later I was told of the great rejoicing when plumbing finally came to the rock. The privy over the precipice had probably caused more than one lighthouse keeper to change his occupation, and later on, I was to learn why.

In the kitchen, or the galley (a personal choice of the individual), I encountered Allik once again and pried him with questions. He had his hands full preparing the evening meal and I assumed he was the regular cook. When informed that each keeper took his turn on a rotation basis, I nearly swallowed my tongue. I couldn't even boil water and make it come out right. The kitchen was simple a stove that could cook and heat the room, old wooden cupboards, a plain table and four stiff-backed chairs. A small pantry was attached to the room, and for all intents and purposes this area was the center of the social activities for this stationary rock-bottomed ship. A desk of sorts for light-house business and for entries in the lighthouse log was kept in plain sight.

Entered George, the potentate. In rather gruff terms he informed me watches were kept around the clock. The light was turned on an hour before sunset and turned off an hour after sunrise. Whenever the weather thickened and the visibility was less than two miles, the foghorn was activated. Hourly inspections were made night and day, and every afternoon except Sunday, the complete routine of lighthouse cleaning was pursued. Maintenance of mach-inery was a necessity, and exterior painting was done when weather conditions warranted. Most things were in duplicate-foghorns, compressors, generators and electrical systems. A standby kerosene lamp was available for placement in the lens should the electrical systems short out. Three keepers stood eight-hour watches; the cook did his own thing.

"Yah got the midnight watch," said George, "and," he added, "Yah better not fall asleep."

Without hesitation he proceeded to show me the "ropes," as he called them.

Before returning to my room I made a final inspection of my new home, climbing up the spiral staircase that entered into a watch room. Cold and damp, it had a huge iron storm door that led to an outside gallery. Another small iron staircase took me up to the lantern room where stood a huge eight-eyed areo-marine beacon, which I was to learn later was installed after a howling 1934 southwesterly gale had shattered the glass prisms of the lighthouse's original first-order French-made lens. I could not believe it when told that seas sometimes leaped 134 feet to the top of the lantern, breaking the window panes, the lens prisms and filling the tower's interior with rocks and debris.

Areo-Marine Beacon
Light range 17 miles

First Order Fresnel Lens
Light range 22 miles

There I stood alone surveying this strange hunk of real estate that had defied the block-busting ocean ramparts for untold years. Men had challenged and conquered this conical mass many decades earlier, placing a sentinel atop its crest. As I looked down into the gray gloom of sea and sky, dusk slowly settled in. The ocean hissed and rolled, slashing mercilessly against the base of the rock, and the winds whistled around the circular lantern house in weird crescendos. I felt even lonelier than before; it was like a bad dream that would soon end, but instead, it was only the beginning.

Soon it would be time for the bulging glass-eyed monster to start its slow rotation, sending 80,000 candle-power flashes of light to sea, warning of the dangers of this basaltic obstruction off Oregon's salty coast. It gave one a humanitarian feeling, yet at the moment, my inner feelings were anything but along that line. I was suddenly shocked out of my mood when the powerful roar of the foghorn deafened my ears. The weather had closed in and the guttural sound permeated the entire structure. What had I gotten myself into?

Chapter Fourteen
TALES OF TILLY: A NIGHT OF HORROR
by James A. Gibbs

The first evening meal gave me a chance to get to know my cell mates better. Ill at ease, I entered the kitchen where I found eager eaters ready to sink their choppers into Allik's delicacies. Steaming serving dishes were filled with boiled potatoes, vegetables and some type of meat that I couldn't readily identify.

"Okay," said the cook, "eat up."

George sat down like a sack of walnuts, his joints creaking. Allik was much gentler in his approach. The third keeper, whom I had seen in the derrick house, was Roy Dibb, who proved much more sociable than the others. I was soon to learn that his greatest joy in life was golfing, most of his spare leave being spent at the Astoria Country Club, where he consistently shot in the low eighties or high seventies, despite his ripening age.

George's table manners left a little to be desired, perhaps because his false teeth didn't fit too well. Still, he could really stow it away.

"Pass the bread," he demanded, his mouth opening like a cargo hatch. As Roy pushed the plate his way, two slices were swept off with a single stroke.

Allik watched his culinary efforts pass into oblivion. I was thankful I didn't feel very hungry for I might have had to struggle for my fair share. Even the jello dessert vanished in short order.

As the Tillamook crew slurped down their coffee among belches and teeth picking, the conversation somehow got around to the subject of the lighthouse ghost. On certain nights, strange unexplained noises were heard in the tower, they informed me. I was certain these old foxes were trying to frighten a young man as a sort of lighthouse initiation, but then I had always scoffed at such nonsense.

As I was later to learn, every "genuine" lighthouse boasted of having a ghost, some legitimate, others illegitimate, if such terminology can be used. Keepers often heard unseen, unexplained footsteps, saw materials moved around, oil lamps blown out mysteriously and windows and doors left ajar. For some strange reason, ghosts and ghouls seem to favor the architecture of a lighthouse. The solitude and privation leaves a fertile field for the over-active mind. As for the Tillamook wraith, I would have to draw my own conclusion.

Feeling quite exhausted after dinner, I parted company in anticipation of the midnight watch. Going to my room, I gently closed the door, un-dogged the porthole and let a strong sea breeze blow fresh air into my stuffy domicile. I took in some deep breaths and proceeded to undress. Turning out the light, I flopped into bed and pulled up the covers. The springs dug into my back through a worn-out mattress and for an hour or so I tossed and turned while thinking over the events of the day. I was thankful the foghorn had ceased blowing, but I could think of nothing else to cheer me at the moment.

Finally I dozed off, but shortly after awakened with a start. I was positive I heard footsteps in the room and instantly sprang up to a 90-degree angle. The nerves in my body tensed. Then I remembered the order about keepers not entering another's room. Momentarily relaxing, I assured myself that it was only the pranks of a freshening wind and a restless sea. When I had nearly convinced myself, there was another step, even closer. The light switch was at the other end of the room, but my body suddenly stiffened. How much did I actually know about these strange lighthouse keepers? Was there really a ghost in the tower?

For some reason I just couldn't move. I pinched myself to be sure it wasn't a nightmare, but this was no dream, it was real. I grew rigid all over again and tried to call out, but the utterances seemed to choke in my throat. After hearing two more steps, I knew that whatever it was, was standing next to my bed. Then came that terrifying moment when something passed near my throat, so close that the breeze fanned my face.

Visions of a knife, of violent pain, and warm blood seized me. In the awful darkness, my body suddenly acted from instinct. Swinging my arms wildly with my every ounce of my strength, I leaped from my bed, pillow in front of my face, and charged my attacker like a Notre Dame fullback. Then something tripped me and I went sprawling across the floor. Slamming into the wall, I struck my head and sank my fingernails into the plaster while trying to regain my feet. I felt around in confused haste for the light switch. My heart was beating like a trip hammer and it seemed an eternity before the dim globe came to life.

Turning to face my assailant, I nearly collapsed on seeing what was there. A mammoth goose with a broken wing sat in the middle of the floor. Evidently blinded by the beacon, it had flown through the open porthole and broken its wing en route. Each wing flap had resembled a human footstep, and the most dreaded moment must have occurred when the goose leaped up on the chair beside my bed and flapped its wing next to my throat.

The strenuous ordeal left me rigid. I didn't know whether to laugh, cry or scream. Finally I swooped up the bird, which until that moment had made no vocal sounds. Marching him straight outside to the cadence of his honking, I dropped him with a plunk in a sheltered corner of the lighthouse and made haste back to my warm bed to capitalize on a well-earned sleep.

Never was that phantom goose seen again. For all I know he may have walked off the edge of the rock and ended it all. I will confess, however, that if the goose had not been there when I flipped on the light I would indeed have become a staunch believer in ghosts.

My deep sleep was interrupted rudely with a loud pounding on the door. "Your watch!" said the knocker. After dressing, I made my way to the kitchen where George waited to be relieved.

"What's a matter with yah?" he questioned. "Yah look like you seen a ghost."

For a moment I thought he was psychic, but then I was too embarrassed to tell him what had happened. Besides, he looked tired and eager for bed. As he got up to leave, he turned with a furrowed brow, gruffly stating, "Half-hour checks on everything."

I nodded, then suddenly found myself alone in the kitchen with four walls staring at me. I looked up at the old Regulator clock on the wall, which slowly ticked away the minutes. When the time came for my first rounds, I went outside into the cold, windy night to check the visibility. The atmosphere had cleared somewhat and a slight drizzle pricked my face. The roar the sea was intense and all around was a black abyss, except when the probing beams of light from the beacon cut the darkness like a knife. For obvious reasons it was scary outside and I was glad to re-enter the fog signal house.

Continuing my rounds, I headed for the tower and began climbing the spiral staircase to check the light. As I ascended, my shoes clattered against the iron grates. The sounds called back at me, echoing off the tower walls. Just before I reached the watch room, I detected another unrelated noise, strange, haunting. Stopping in my tracks, I stood motionless. There it was again, a whispering moan, like one in pain.

"Oh, not again," thought I to myself. The goose was all I could take for one night. But this was different, and the utterance smacked of something human. Could one of the keepers be trying to frighten me? "Oh, you foolish soul," thought I. These old duffers had better things to do than go around playing ghost. Then I got to thinking of the conversation at the dinner table. Were there really such wraiths, I wondered, or were they only a figment of the imagination. I looked all around trying to figure out the source of those strange sounds but could draw no logical conclusion. Thus I hastily parted company with the unseen apparition, scurried into the watch room and then climbed the ladder to the lamp room.

Great flashes of light caused spectrums of color on the wall as the lens turned silently in its carriage. I didn't dare look directly into the beam, so intense was the light source. The reflectors directed the beams 18 miles to sea. As instructed, I took the stop watch and timed the characteristic-one flash every 5 seconds, 0.8 second flash. As far as I could determine with my neophyte lighthouse knowledge, the lens and its electric motor were in excellent shape, doing accurately the job for which they were designed.

Now at last, for just a brief moment, I felt a slight bit useful. Here I was in the "crown room" of old Tillamook Rock Light house, checking the light that beamed its warnings to vessels at sea. Wiping some specks of dust from the lantern panes, I felt bathed in light rays as the flashes fleeted by like dancing nymphs. It was a kind of warm feeling. Out of curiosity, I stopped the lens carriage and opened a metal door to check on one of two 500-watt globes which seemed to be burning with all its heart. Then I noticed some of the marks on the half deck where the former first order lens and lightning apparatus had been cradled, before the fury of the Pacific did its destruction twelve years earlier. As I was later to learn, the lens had been one of the most beautiful at any Pacific light station-hundreds of hand ground prisms created by a French manufacturer and mounted in a specially made brass framework. For all the world, when illuminated it had been like a monstrous diamond, glistening and glowing in a myriad of color and lucidity.

An oil lamp was once used inside the old lens, a large glass chimney attached to carry the smoke up to the ball-shaped opening in the lantern-house roof. When the lamp was lighted, it sent its diverse rays into powerful beams by refracting the character of the prisms, each one at a different angle, a formula worked out years earlier by the eminent French scientist, Augustin Fresnel. For decades his discoveries gave the French a premier role as manufacturers of lighthouse lenses and related equipment.

It was a sad day at Tillamook when the original apparatus was removed, replaced by an American-made aero-marine beacon. To the mariner at sea, however, only the characteristic and the intensity of the light mattered, not its history.

I started back down the ladder, satisfied that all was well in the lamp room. Suddenly my thoughts were diverted back to the ghost in the tower. Sure enough, those same sounds were again audible in the same area. I was certain the three keepers were fast asleep at that hour, so it was just the spook and me. Then my eyes fell on a small door near the landing which I had evidently overlooked in surveying the lighthouse. Going back to the kitchen to get a flashlight, I returned to investigate. Could it be that the strange noises were coming from behind that door?

As if playing a role in a mystery movie, I automatically tiptoed toward the entrance. My hand reached for the handle. Timorous, I stepped back as it creaked open. Gathering myself composure, I bolted inside. The air was dank and there was barely enough headroom to stand erect. As I flashed the light around, shadows played on the wall like hobgoblins around a witch's brew.

Finally I found a light bulb on the ceiling and pulled a protruding chain. At first it didn't respond, but finally a dim glow flooded the room which, as I was later to learn, had been created after the original metal lighthouse roof had been holed repeatedly by sea-thrown boulders. It was a storage area of sorts and a place to keep books sent from mainlanders who related to the lonely role of the lighthouse keepers. From the looks of the place nobody ever used it; cobwebs were everywhere. It was like the attic of an early American residence, with a littering of castoffs. What a perfect home for the lighthouse ghost-and certainly a shadowy hideaway that needed future scrutiny. The floor creaked but the moaning sounds I heard in the tower were not in that room. As the flashlight fell across the sagging bookshelves, I removed two volumes and returned to the more pleasant surroundings of the kitchen.

Making my entry in the log, I sat down to study the literary gems I had taken from the upper room. Blowing a collection of dust from the first, I discovered the auspicious title, Tom Swift and the Motor Cycle. Casting it aside, I picked up the other, which told about the old U.S. Lighthouse Service and some of its problems. I thumbed through to an article on the Navassa Lighthouse on a rock pile in the Caribbean and-wouldn't you know on this night of all nights, there was an account of the supernatural. Inasmuch as it was an isolated sea girt lighthouse like Tillamook, my curiosity was naturally aroused and I read on. It went something like this:

The head keeper was an individual of 20 years' experience in lighthouses, quiet, practical and certainly not a believer in supernatural things. He was chosen to handle the station after oppressive heat and miserable privation had delayed its completion till 1917. There was an indescribable something about that small island on the sea road to Panama (near Haiti and Cuba), rumor persisting that it was cursed, a holdover from the days when black laborers with white overlords off-loaded its guano resources. A mutiny among the workers had created a blood bath in which several were killed.

That first evening, the keeper-in-charge ascended the tower staircase (just as I had done that very night) and became conscious of the reverberating sound of his feet on the grates. After tending the light and while returning to the dwelling for coffee, he was aware of the damp, humid night, despite a clear, star-laden sky. Then he heard it-a low, rhythmic wailing sound coming from outside, a sound resembling a man with a high-pitched voice accompanied by a shallow drum. Not believing in spooks and such trivia, despite having served in several lighthouses all claiming ghosts, he believed in a logical explanation for everything. Still, curiosity prompted the keeper to open the door and listen until the whistling wind finally drowned out the sound.

Nevertheless he took his lantern and inspected the area. Satisfied that no intruders were about, he started back. When he reached the dwelling, a loud cackling laugh from the sea pierced his ears. Believing it a strange combination of shrieking sea birds, he dismissed it from his mind not sharing the experience with his assistant.

Two nights passed without consequence. On the third, it happened again. The keeper distinctly heard the same dull throbbing of the drum. While his assistant was winding the weights that turned the lens, he stole silently out into the night. Scurrying toward a clump of wild growth a short distance from the lighthouse, he hid himself from sight. Again the drums began beating, slowly and silently at first, then gaining momentum and volume. The pulsating beat was mingled with the cry of birds and the incessant wind.

Then came the same haunting voice that had startled him the first night, this time in a chant. The words sounded like, "Go 'way, white man, go 'way befo' too late!"

It was the call of one troubled, seemingly warning of impending doom. But how could this be? There was nobody else on the island but the two attendants of the lighthouse.

He wondered if the oppressive island possessed some strange mysticism. The tempo grew into a wild chant, the apparent warning continuing with greater rapidity as the drums grew ever louder.

While the listener crouched in the thick growth, the chanter's message, in broken English, seemed to be telling of the brutality heaped upon the blacks before the awful Navassa riot of yesteryear. Numbed by it all, the keeper made no attempt to capture his taunter nor was he able to see any clear image. Instead, each night when not on duty, he returned to his secluded listening post to hear the chant. The entire episode smacked of voodoo, and this the keeper knew, but try as he would he could not resist the strange magnetic pull. The keeper became progressively morose and nervous. Alarmed by such behavior, the assistant watched his superior stare for hours on end at the vast sea, tapping his fingers on the table in the same tempo as the voodoo drums. Sometimes he was incoherent, neglecting his duties.

One day, as if in a trance, the troubled man came back to the lighthouse pale as a ghost, chanting a strange jargon and beating his chest in drum-like rhythm. He was stark mad.

By running up distress flags, his frantic associate was able to attract a passing ship. But after signals were exchanged the vessel sailed away and it was two harrowing weeks before a lighthouse tender arrived off the island to remove the demented keeper.

The drums were then suddenly silenced and the voodoo chant was heard no more, nor was its originator, if any, ever found.

For a decade after the incident, the Lighthouse Service maintained personnel at the station, but few could stand the awful privation, the bloodsucking insects and fever. Voodoo rumors persisted all the while.

Finally, in 1929, the Lighthouse Service authorities threw in the sponge, admitting that Navassa was not fit for human habitation. The lighthouse was in turn automated at considerable expense and is still operated with occasional servicing from a buoy tender out of Miami.

It was almost ironic that I should come across such an article on my first night as a lighthouse keeper. I was careful, thereafter, not to take the ghost of Tillamook lightly.

It was one of the longest nights of my life, but finally out of the east a pale glow appeared over towering Tillamook Head, a giant monolith rising from the mainland beach a mile or so east of the rock. A sea mist hung low and the ocean had calmed somewhat.

Through the night I had imagined all kinds of things in the shadows and none of them seemed pleasant-clammy, wet, miserable things the kind that make one wish for desert sunshine. In the days that followed, strange and ghostly visitations were seriously discussed and often considered as omens to be heeded. For some reason, lighthouses seem to spawn more than their share of ghostly tales and supernatural happenings.

My entry in the lighthouse log that morning was routine, for who would have believed my experiences of that night?

Author James Gibbs at
Lighthouse Front Door

Chapter Fifteen   Tilly Trivia

- The Tillamook Lighthouse was the third lighthouse protecting the entrance to the Columbia River. The others were Cape Disappointment and Point Adams.

- The lighthouse is located one mile off shore from the Tillamook Head, just south of Seaside Oregon.

Photo: Neal Maine ©Pacific Light Images

- The lighthouse lantern room, with its Fresnel lens light, stood 135 feet above the ocean.

- Navigation aids along rivers were tended on a part-time basis by local citizens called Lamp Lighters or Lamp Attendants.

- During the construction of the lighthouse, only one life was lost. A master mason from Portland slipped on the wet, slimy Rock and fell into the ocean. His body was never recovered.

139

- Sea conditions building the Tillamook Rock Lighthouse were often brutal, so brutal that local workers could not be found to work on the lighthouse, which many called a 'hoodoo light.'

- Work officially started on the lighthouse on October 26, 1879. The first structure built on the Rock was a reverse-flow outhouse that clung on the precipice of the island like a conical shell, 90 feet directly over the ocean.

- Lighthouse Keepers were called 'wickies' because they trimmed and lit the wicks of the lighthouse beacons. Kerosene was the fuel of choice for lighthouse Keepers.

- Reporting for work on the Rock required the lighthouse Keepers to ride the derrick from ship to shore.

- In July of 1934, two men swam nine miles in the frigid Pacific Ocean, from the Seaside turn-around to the Tillamook Rock Lighthouse. The lighthouse Keepers welcomed the swimmers with hot baths, coffee, and a hardy breakfast.

- In 1939, two of the oldest Government maritime services were combined: the U. S. Coast Guard and the U. S. Lighthouse Service.

- The single most expensive item on the Rock was the Fresnel lens in the tower lantern room.

- The most expensive construction item was the cost of ships and crews for transportation of personnel, building materials, and supplies to the Rock.

- The explosives used to decapitate the top of the monolith consumed over 1500 pounds of black powder.

- The ashlar stone used in the construction of the lighthouse was quarried from Mount Tabor in Portland, Oregon. It is the same type of stone used by the Incan Empire to build the wall at Machu Picchu.

- The island was the nastiest chunk of rubble anywhere in the world. On January 21, 1881, after 575 days of work, the light came on. Total cost to build the station was $123,493.

- The Rock is split in two by a narrow fissure where the seas rush in like an express train, exploding with ear-shattering roars and shooting skyward in great geysers.

Photo: Neal Maine ©Pacific Light Images

- First Head Keeper was Albert Roeder. The last Head Keeper was Oswald Allik.

- In the 77 years of its operation, there is no record that any woman ever set foot in the Tillamook Rock Lighthouse.

- Today, the island is a Federal Wildlife Refuge, a National Historic site and privately owned.

- It's a morbid reality but this bleak Alcatraz for souls still has urns of remains inside the old station, 'Honorary Lighthouse Keepers' as Eternity at Sea called them.

- Someday, sometime, this bastion-like structure will succumb to the tempests of the Pacific.

- It wasn't uncommon for whales and sharks to visit the base of the lighthouse monolith and, under the proper conditions, rub off barnacles and other crustaceans, using the rough rocks deep within the fissure. The whales were mostly California Grays.

- There is no ledger or record of how many lives Tillamook Rock Lighthouse saved during her 77 year career. The number most likely is in the thousands, if not more.

- There are an estimated 680 lighthouses remaining in the U.S. The East Coast has 391 lighthouses, the Gulf and Great Lake states 195 and the West Coast has 94

- Tillamook Rock Lighthouse is now closed to the public but visible from the Oregon coastal cities of Seaside, Cannon Beach as well as Ecola State Park.

A lightship is a ship which acts as a lighthouse and used in waters that are too deep or otherwise unsuitable for lighthouse construction. Commissioned in 1951, the Lightship Columbia, WLV-604, was the fourth and final lightship stationed at the mouth of the Columbia River. The new ship replaced the aging vessel LV-93, which had been in service since 1939. The lightships guided vessels across the Columbia River Bar and an area known as the 'Graveyard of the Pacific', from 1892 until 1979. Columbia was the final lightship to serve on the west coast. She was replaced by an automated navigational buoy soon after, which has since been retired.

While in service, the Lightship Columbia had a permanent 18 man crew stationed on board, consisting of 17 enlisted men and one warrant officer who served as the ship's Captain. Everything the crew needed had to be on board. In the winter, weeks of rough weather prevented any supplies from being delivered. Life on board the lightship was marked by long stretches of monotony and boredom, intermixed with riding out gale force storms.

The retired Lightship Columbia is now moored in Astoria, Oregon at the docks of the Columbia River Maritime Museum, alongside the navigational buoy that replaced her in 1979. Visitors are welcome aboard, for tours on the Lightship Columbia.

Top: Machine room during Tillamook station operations.
Bottom: Same machine room years after decommissioning

ACKNOWLEDGMENTS

There is an old marketing adage, 'find the need and fill the need.' These words ring so true about this book project. When Karen Emmerling, the proprietor of Beach Books in Seaside, Oregon, told me about her frustration of finding a book on the history of Tillamook Rock Lighthouse, a light (so to speak!) turned on in my head. Seems the last two books on the subject were long out of print: '*Tillamook Light*', by James A. Gibbs (last published 1979) and '*Terrible Tilly*', by Bert Webber (last published 1992). A book about this relic of a lighthouse was one of the tourists most requested topics. So my thanks to Karen (and 'AB'☺) for her encouragement to pen this history.

This project was a joy to research and develop. Using the old out of print books as reference and including new information, stories and photos resulting from personal interviews, in depth research at various museums, libraries, newspapers, government agencies and the web, this book took shape. It's my honor to dedicate this book to James Gibbs, who worked as a Keeper on the Rock and first wrote of the Tillamook Lighthouse decades ago. Personal thanks to his family, daughter Deb and her husband Ray, who allowed me to use some of Jim's words, stories and generously provided me with some of Jim's personal lighthouse photo collection. Jim loved the old lighthouse, I hope he would approve of my endeavor to tell its story.

Special thanks to photographer Neal Maine at Pacific Light Images, who shared with us his spectacular pictures of the lighthouse today. His gift of crafting images is exceptional. Other photographs in this book were licensed from museums, came from private collections, were provided by government agencies, were public domain or found on the internet, all without embedded copyright notices. If this publisher has inadvertently infringed on any copyrights, please give notice and the material will be removed in forthcoming editions.
Thanks also to Kathleen at KP Graphics.

Hat's off to my long-time story editor Judy Meyers who helped me with many of the stories contained within and to Katie Miller who edited and proofed the manuscript. These professional editors make me look better with their special talents for the English language. As always, love and gratitude to my wife Tess, my favorite editor!

<u>Special Thanks to the Staff, Volunteers at:</u>

Cannon Beach History Center and Museum
Clatsop County Historical Society: Heritage Museum
Columbia River Maritime Museum
Oregon Coast History Center
Seaside Museum and Historical Society
Seaside Public Library
Seaside Signal Newspaper
Tillamook County Library
Tillamook County Pioneer Museum
United States Lighthouse Society

About the Author

Brian D. Ratty is a retired media executive, publisher and graduate of Brooks Institute of Photography. He and his wife, Tess, live on the north Oregon Coast, where he writes and photographs that rugged and majestic region. Over the past thirty five years, he has traveled the vast wilderness of the Pacific Coast in search of images and stories that reflect the spirit and splendor of those spectacular lands. Brian is an award-winning historical fiction author of six novels and the owner of Sunset Lake Publishing.

For more information: DutchClarke.com and
Facebook.com/Dutch1942

Books by Brian Ratty

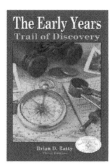

DC1
The Early Years: Trail of Discovery (Third Edition)
ISBN-13: 978-0692254721
114,348 words - 304 pages
Retail: $20.00
Foreword Magazine: Book of the Year Finalist
Amazon Breakthrough Novel Awards: Quarter Finalist
If you enjoyed Jack London's classic 'Call of the Wild,'
you'll love The Early Years.

DC2
The War Years: Through A Bloody Lens (Second Edition)
ISBN-13: 978-0615987286
173,819 words - 472 pages
Retail: $20.00
Foreword Magazine: Book of the Year
Eric Hoffer Award-Winner
With the flavor of The Band of Brothers and the substance
of Saving Private Ryan, don't miss The War Years!

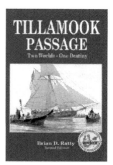

DC3
Tillamook Passage: Two Worlds – One Destiny
ISBN-13: 978-0692259351
131,834 words - 358 Pages
Retail: $20.00
Eric Hoffer Award-winner
Tillamook Passage is a rare view of the life and
times of the Oregon Coastal Indians

Available at fine book stores and online
For more Information:
DutchClarke.com

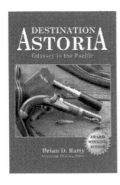

DC4
Destination Astoria: Odyssey to the Pacific
ISBN-13: 978-0615940779
161,000 words – 437 pages
Retail: $20.00
5 stars, Readers' Favorite
If you enjoyed the classic novel 'The Last of the Mohicans,' you will love Destination Astoria.

DC5
Voyage of Atonement: The Tainted Treasure
ISBN-13: 978-0692454282
140,000 words - 390 pages
Retail: $20.00
5 stars, Readers' Favorite
Rich in atmosphere and characters, this is a thrilling story of war buddies that navigate the Pacific in search of the past.

DC6
Over the Next Horizon: In Retrospect
ISBN-13: 978-0692847459
56,000 words – 154 pages
Retail: $15.00
There are no shortcuts through the wilderness of life. Over the Next Horizon is a commentary of our common history and a retrospect of our life and times.

Sunset Lake Publishing LLC
Sunsetlakepublishing.com

Made in the USA
Monee, IL
16 January 2024